LO... ...ND
SOCIAL CHOICE

MONOGRAPHS IN MODERN LOGIC

edited by

G. B. KEENE

LOGIC AND SOCIAL CHOICE

BY

Y. Murakami

LONDON: Routledge & Kegan Paul Ltd
NEW YORK: Dover Publications Inc

First published 1968
in Great Britain by
Routledge & Kegan Paul Ltd
Broadway House, 68–74 Carter Lane
London, E.C.4
and in the USA by
Dover Publications Inc
180 Varick Street
New York, 10014

Library of Congress Catalog Card Number: 67–26965

SBN 7100 2981 0

Printed in Great Britain
by Richard Clay (The Chaucer Press), Ltd.,
Bungay, Suffolk

CONTENTS

Contents

Chapter One

INTRODUCTION

1. Society and Individuals. A society consists of individual members and a society's decision is composed of its members' decisions. Each society has its own rule for making decisions. When a combination of individual decisions is given, a society's decision is reached according to that rule. Probably the most familiar example of a social decision-making rule is *voting*. By casting a ballot, each individual expresses his decision on the issue in question, say, an election where a Conservative candidate and a Labour candidate are contesting a seat in Parliament. Society adopts the decision supported by the majority of voters; thus, if the Conservative candidate obtains more votes, he is the 'social choice'. Once a pattern of individual decisions is formed, the rule of majority voting yields a social decision. As the pattern changes, the social decision also varies. The mathematician, as well as the logician, would say that a social decision is a *function* of individual decisions, in the sense that a combination of individual decisions determines a social decision. More formally, we may express this as

$$R = F(R_1, R_2, \ldots, R_n)$$

where R and R_j are variables for the decisions of the

1

society and of the jth individual respectively, n being the number of individuals. The function F represents society's rule for decision-making, so we may call this function the *social decision function*.

Any change in a social decision can occur only through changes in individual decisions. Thus, by the formulation presented above we can express any social decision-making rule. Sometimes, as in the case of religious taboos, a social decision may be traditionally fixed, regardless of changes in individual decisions. However, a traditionally fixed social decision is still a function of individual decisions, in the sense that the function takes on a constant value. In some societies, a particular individual may be so powerful that his decision is always adopted by the society. In other words, the individual is a dictator. But this dictatorial rule of social decision-making constitutes simply a special class of social decision function; individuals other than the dictator can be deleted from the function. Whether a society is traditional, dictatorial or democratic, which we shall investigate later, the social decision function as defined above is sufficiently general to express any form of social decision.

2. Individual Decisions. From a psychological point of view, an individual decision is a complex phenomenon. Hedonist psychology assumes that an individual decision is a revelation of the person's desire, satisfaction, pleasure, taste or whatever the philosopher or social scientist wishes to call it. Many economic analyses, as well as the utilitarian philosophy behind them, are known to be based on a similar view. On the other hand, many people argue that the exercise of individual desire is restrained by some idealistic

principle, or perhaps by some subconscious motiva-
tion. The question of how and why individual
decisions are made belongs to the field of psychology.

Throughout this book we shall be concerned with
the 'behaviouristic' rather than the motivational aspect
of decision making. By an *individual decision* we mean
simply that the individual behaves as if he had a
definite order of preference concerning the *alternatives*
open to him. Whatever his motivations, the individual
behaves as if he had arranged, in his mind, all the
conceivable alternatives, in order of preference, when
he makes a decision. This is our definition of individual
decision.

Mr. Smith, a citizen in a Midwest town, prefers a
Republican candidate to a Democratic candidate for
some reason of his own. This is his decision. Mr.
Jones, a gentleman in North Devon, prefers a Liberal
candidate to a Conservative candidate, and a Conservative candidate to a Labour candidate. Various
motivations prompt Mr. Jones to make this decision.
One of the most fundamental assumptions of economics is that a consumer orders all possible expenditure
plans according to his preference. The well-known
'indifference map' is a device to describe visually a
consumer's ordering. Each individual's indifference
map reveals his decision.

Throughout this book, we shall generally regard an
individual's *decision* as equivalent to his *preference*,
represented as an *ordering*, or, in short, to his *preference ordering*. It must be noted, however, that a
distinction between *preference* and *decision* is sometimes meaningful. For an individual may sometimes
purposely misrepresent his preference ordering. Once

a social decision-making rule is given, an individual might find it profitable to misrepresent his preference in action. That is, he might act *insincerely*. We shall assume in this book, however, that every individual is *sincere* or, in other words, that every individual's decision is identical with his preference. This is one of the limitations of this book.

However, we shall later present (Section 10, Chapter Four) a condition under which no misrepresentation of individual preference is profitable. We shall see that this condition is satisfied by many social decision functions familiar to us; so we may sometimes be justified in assuming individual sincerity. Only in that section, are decision and preference to be carefully distinguished. Otherwise, both terms will be employed interchangeably.

Indeed, the concept of decision can be formulated in many other ways with greater sophistication. For example, we may include not only preference orders but also preference intensities as elements of an individual decision. In fact, we shall examine this idea in Chapter Six. Or we may assume that preference itself is subject to uncertainty; the reader interested in this 'probability' approach may refer to R. D. Luce's work (a). However, in this introductory book we shall start with the most elementary assumption that decision is preference ordering.

3. Axioms of Ordering. An individual decision has now been defined as an individual preference ordering of all conceivable alternatives. In this section we shall formulate a preference ordering in exact logical terms. We shall start by denoting *alternatives*, or possible states of the society, by lower-case letters $x, y, z, \ldots$.

4

Introduction

We assume that there is a basic set of alternatives which could conceivably be presented to every individual as well as to the society. This set of all conceivable alternatives may be called an *issue* and denoted by capital S.

For example, in the U.S. presidential election of 1964, the issue consisted of two elements, Johnson and Goldwater. In some constituency in England in an election year—say, in North Devon in 1965—the issue may consist of three elements: a Labour candidate, a Conservative candidate and a Liberal candidate

An issue does not necessarily consist of immediately available alternatives, as in the last two examples. For example, if we are concerned with the North Devon constituency, but not confined to the election of 1965, we can conceive infinitely many alternatives in an infinite horizon; some candidate may change his platform, or be replaced by another candidate, or some other party may enter the election. Thus an issue of such a general nature may include infinitely many alternatives, whether immediately available or remotely conceivable. This book will not be particularly concerned with the availability of alternatives; availability is, after all, a relative concept. In any case, let us start by assuming that an issue is somehow defined.

For any given issue, a decision or a preference ordering may be visualized as a 'relation' among alternatives in it. Moreover, we shall show in the following that a preference ordering is primarily a relation between two alternatives or, in logical terms, a *binary* or *dyadic relation*.

Let us consider a pair of alternatives (x, y) taken in

5

this order. Concerning the pair (x, y), the j-th individual's decision takes one of the following three forms: he prefers alternative x to alternative y, he prefers y to x, or he neither prefers x to y, nor y to x. In order to express the first two possible forms, we may introduce, for convenience's sake, the binary relation xP_jy which symbolizes the statement that the jth individual prefers alternative x to alternative y. A binary relation xP_jy may be called a *preference relation* of the jth individual; such a preference relation should be distinguished from a preference ordering, of which a preference relation is a part.

For a given pair of alternatives (x, y), the jth individual may prefer x to y, or he may not prefer x to y. Thus xP_jy does hold or does not hold, depending on a pair of alternatives (x, y) taken in this order. If x and y are thought of as variables, each of which runs over a set S, then xP_jy may be regarded as a two-place predicate, in terms of logic. If all the rules of deduction in predicate logic are assumed, we can set up a logical calculus of relations, as in ordinary predicate logic. Throughout this book, we assume all those rules of deduction required to develop such a calculus of relational logic.

In order to express essential features of a preference ordering, we may now impose the following well-known axioms, which are, in fact, common to all ordering relations.

Axiom 1 (irreflexivity of preference): xP_jx does not hold for any alternative x:

$$(x) \sim xP_jx$$

Axiom 1' (anti-symmetry of preference): For any

pair of alternatives (x, y), if xP_jy holds, then yP_jx does not hold:

$$(x)(y) \sim (xP_jy \,.\, yP_jx)$$

Axiom 2 (transitivity of preference): For any triple of alternatives (x, y, z), if xP_jy and yP_jz hold, then xP_jz holds:

$$(x)(y)(z)\{(xP_jy \,.\, yP_jz) \supset xP_jz\}$$

As is easily verified, either Axiom 1 or Axiom 1′ can be derived from the remaining two axioms. We have two equivalent formulations of the axioms of preference—Axioms 1 and 2, or Axioms 1′ and 2.

As we mentioned before, a preference relation is not the only possible type of decision concerning a pair of alternatives. The remaining possibility is that an individual neither prefers x to y nor y to x. In other words, he is *indifferent* between x and y; in his decision, an alternative x 'is indifferent to' an alternative y. Let us now define the binary relation xI_jy as equivalent to $\{\sim xP_jy \,.\, \sim yP_jx\}$; this is a symbolization of the statement that the jth individual is indifferent between x and y. A binary relation xI_jy may be called an *indifference relation* of the jth individual.

Several properties immediately follow from this definition of an indifference relation.

Theorem 1–1 (connectedness): For any pair of alternatives (x, y), one and only one of the following holds: xP_jy, xI_jy, yP_jx.

Theorem 1–2 (reflexivity of indifference): For any alternative x, xI_jx holds:

$$(x)xI_jx$$

7

Theorem 1–3 (symmetry of indifference): For any pair of alternatives (x, y), xI_jy holds if and only if yI_jx holds:

$$(x)(y)(xI_jy \equiv yI_jx)$$

The reader can now verify that, under Axioms 1 and 2, all alternatives are arranged in a kind of 'ordering'. However, this 'ordering' cannot rank the alternatives in a complete way. For, even if x is indifferent to y, and y is indifferent to z, x may be, for example, preferred to z. We cannot find any way of ranking three alternatives x, y, z in one order of preference. It should be noted that an indifference relation defined thus far can be interpreted even as a mere incomparability in the sense that the jth individual is incapable of comparing two alternatives in question. A binary relation under Axioms 1 and 2 results in only a 'partial' ordering.

Therefore, we generally assume in this book:

Axiom 3 (transitivity of indifference): For any triple of alternatives (x, y, z), if xI_jy and yI_jz hold, then xI_jz holds:

$$(x)(y)(z)\{(xI_jy \cdot yI_jz) \supset xI_jz\}$$

Any binary relation which is reflexive, symmetric and transitive is usually called an *equivalence relation*, which plays the same role in relational logic as an equality plays in mathematics. An indifference relation is now required to be an equivalence relation. It can be seen that all alternatives are now classified into disjoint and mutually exclusive classes such that any two alternatives in the same class are mutually indifferent and any two alternatives from two different classes are never mutually indifferent. A preference ordering on all alternatives is now reduced to a preference relation on all those *equivalence classes*. All alternatives are completely ordered on a scale of preference. A binary relation under Axioms 1, 2 and 3 is a 'complete' ordering.

With the help of Axiom 3 we now have:

Theorem 1-4: For any triple of alternatives (x, y, z), if xI_jy and yP_jz hold, then xP_jz holds, and if xP_jy and yI_jz hold, then xP_jz holds:

$$(x)(y)(z)\{(xI_jy \cdot yP_jz) \supset xP_jz\},$$
and $$(x)(y)(z)\{(xP_jy \cdot yI_jz) \supset xP_jz\}$$

Axiom 3 is essential to this result. A binary relation satisfying Axioms 1, 2 and 3 is generally called an 'ordering', a 'complete ordering' or a 'weak ordering'. Throughout this book, we assume that every individual's decision is represented as an ordering defined on a specified issue or on a set S.

4. Meaning of Axioms. An examination of the meaning of the axioms may be useful. Axiom 1 or 1' is obviously an essential property of a decision; without this property, a preference relation cannot exist. However, some difference of opinion may arise as to Axiom 2 and Axiom 3. If Axiom 2 does not necessarily hold, a derived relation will give a circular ordering, so to speak. For example, an individual may prefer a Labour candidate to a Conservative and a Conservative to a Liberal, yet he may prefer a Liberal to a Labour candidate. The trouble with this type of decision is that there is no best alternative for the individual. If the word *rationality* means that an individual behaves so as to obtain an alternative best for him, an individual decision violating Axiom 2 cannot be *rational*. By excluding the circular case by virtue of Axiom 2, we assume in this book that every individual is rational in the sense defined above.

As is already mentioned, Axioms 1 and 2 are capable of ordering the alternatives only partially. Some additional axiom is necessary for rendering a partial ordering complete. However, the axiom to be added may not necessarily be Axiom 3. In psychology, the term 'threshold of discrimination', is used in reference to the fact that one can discriminate two things only if their difference is greater than a certain value. Most people can recognize a difference of a half-tone, but few can perceive the difference of a quarter tone or of a one-eighth tone. In the case of a preference ordering, an individual may feel indifferent to a preferential difference between alternative *x* and alternative *y*, as well as to that between *y* and *z*. That is to say, the differences may fall below the individual's threshold of discrimination. However, a difference between *x* and *z* may well be above his threshold. In this case, the individual's indifference relation is not transitive.

This is in fact often the case with ordinary individuals. Although some efforts have been made to analyse an ordering whose indifference relation is *not always* transitive, such an analysis is beyond the scope of this book. The reader interested in further studies may refer, for example, to Rothenberg's argument in Chapter Seven of his book. We shall confine our attention to the more basic case of transitive indifference.

5. Another Axiomatic System of Ordering. We have presented one system of axioms of ordering. There are, however, many ways of formulating the axioms of ordering. As an alternative let us define a binary relation xR_jy as equivalent to $xP_jy \lor xI_jy$:

$$xR_jy \equiv xP_jy \lor xI_jy$$

In verbal terms, xR_jy symbolizes the statement that the jth individual prefers x to y or is indifferent between x and y. Then the following two axioms are equivalent to Axioms 1, 2 and 3:

Axiom I (connectedness): For any pair of alternatives (x, y), xR_jy or yR_jx holds:

$$(x)(y)(xR_jy \lor yR_jx)$$

Axiom II (transitivity): For any triple of alternatives (x, y, z), if xR_jy and yR_jz hold, then xR_jz holds:

$$(x)(y)(z)\{(xR_jy \, . \, yR_jz) \supset xR_jz\}$$

If xP_jy is defined as equivalent to $\sim yR_jx$, an equivalence between two systems can be proved. We may call this binary relation xR_jy a *preference relation* or a *decision* of the jth individual. In this book, we shall freely exchange one axiomatic formulation for another, depending on the occasion.

6. Social Decision. Through exact analogy with an individual decision, we here mean by a *social decision* that a society knows, or behaves as if it knows, what is to be chosen first, what second, third and so on. In other words, a social decision is defined as an ordering defined on an issue; all alternatives are somehow ordered by the society according to its decision-making rule. As with an individual decision, xPy signifies a preference relation of the society, namely, that the society prefers an alternative x to an alternative y. xIy signifies an indifference relation of the society; the society is indifferent between x and y. Then we assume as before:

Axiom 1: $(x) \sim (xPx)$
Axiom 2: $(x)(y)(z)\{(xPy \cdot yPz) \supset xPz\}$
Axiom 3: $(x)(y)(z)\{(xIy \cdot yIz) \supset xIz\}$

It is to be noted that $xIy \equiv (\sim xPy \cdot \sim yPx)$. As before, we might as well assume Axiom 1′, 2 and 3 or Axioms I and II, in place of Axioms 1, 2 and 3. In the case of Axioms I and II, an ordering relation of the society xRy is defined, as before, as equivalent to xPy or xIy.

However, some people may argue that a society's decision is likely to be more whimsical and tends to be less consistent than an individual's decision. In other words, the above system of axioms—probably Axiom 2 and Axiom 3 in particular—might be too strong for a social decision. While fully aware of this criticism, we start by imposing all of Axioms 1, 2 and 3 on any social decision. It will be shown later that this amounts to a heavy imposition on a social decision-making rule. In fact, some types of society *must* violate Axioms 2 and 3. This is one of the main points of this book. The best approach, we believe, is to start by tentatively assuming consistent social decisions, and then to establish the improbability of their consistency.

We are now in a position to conclude the formulation of the *social decision function*. At the very start of a problem, we assume that all individuals as well as the society face a particular *issue* expressed as a well-specified set S of alternatives. Every individual then makes his decision, which can be expressed as an ordering on the set S. The set S covered by a preference ordering of the jth individual may be called an ordered set and conveniently expressed as $\langle S, R_j \rangle$. Similarly let $\langle S, R \rangle$ stand for an ordered set derived by a preference ordering of the society. Then the social decision function is expressed as

$$\langle S, R \rangle = F(\langle S, R_1 \rangle, \langle S, R_2 \rangle, \ldots, \langle S, R_n \rangle)$$

Or, more simply, for a given S.

$$R = F(R_1, R_2, \ldots, R_n)$$

where R_j signifies a preference ordering of the jth individual and R signifies that of the society. This expression is, in fact, the formulation on the first page of this book.

Let us denote by $\Re$ a collection of all conceivable ordered sets derived from S. For example, if the number of alternatives in S is m, then the number of all conceivable ways of ordering is equal to $m! + (m-1)! + \ldots + 2! + 1$, which may be expressed as M. The number of elements in $\Re$ is then equal to M. Generally speaking, the social decision function is a function such that its domain is an n-fold Cartesian product of $\Re$, and its range is the set $\Re$ (where n is the number of individuals). For example, if the number of alternatives is two, so that M is equal to three, the domain of the social decision function is an n-fold Cartesian product of the set $\{xPy, xIy, yPx\}$ and its range is this set itself.

We have now concluded the formulation in our terms of a society and its individuals. By a *society* we mean a group of *individuals* together with some social decision-making rule adopted by them. Thus, a society in the present context can be any such group as

13

the United Nations, the European Economic Community, a nation-state, a local community, a family or a small group of individuals, as long as the respective rule of social decision-making is specified. From our analytical point of view, an analysis of societies can be reduced to an analysis of the logical structures of social decision functions, which we shall carry out in the following chapters.

Suggested Reading

Nidditch, P. H.: *The Development of Mathematical Logic* (1962)

Nidditch, P. H.: *Propositional Calculus* (1962)

Blanche, R.: *Axiomatics* (1962)

Suppes, P.: *Introduction to Logic* (1958)

Rothenberg, J.: *The Measurement of Social Welfare* (1961)

Luce, R. D.: (*a*) *Individual Choice Behavior* (1959)
(*b*) 'Semiorders and a Theory of Utility Discrimination', *Econometrica* (1956)

Chapter Two

SOCIAL DECISION FUNCTION

1. Multiple Alternatives and Multiple Individuals. In this chapter, we shall introduce a logical approach to the analysis of various types of social decision functions. This preliminary section will consider a problem relating to the number of individuals in the society and the number of alternatives in an issue.

If the number of individuals in a society is different from the number of individuals in another society, then obviously two societies are different. It will become apparent in the course of the following argument, however, that from our following analytical point of view, the number of individuals is immaterial, as long as the number remains more than one and finite. A 'society' composed of one individual is obviously trivial. In the case of infinitely many individuals, the social decision functions would have different properties from what they have in the case of a finite number of individuals. Some of the conclusions presented later—particularly the theorem of voting paradox in Chapters Five and Six—cannot be applied to a society of infinitely many individuals. The case is theoretically interesting but evidently of no practical importance, so in this book we shall not be

15

concerned with this infinite case. We are assuming in this book that the number of individuals composing the society is plural and finite. Under this restriction differences in the number of individuals is irrelevant to the following argument.

Another obvious difference concerns types of issues, or of a set S of alternatives. An issue may be any type of set. It may be a subset of a finite-dimensional Euclidean space as in a society composed of consumers, or it may be a space on which no metric is defined. However, a primary difference among various issues is in the numbers of alternatives included in the issues. As we shall later show, a crucial difference exists between the case of two alternatives and the case of more than two alternatives. We may start by considering the case of two alternatives, because every individual or social decision is primarily a binary relation. In the present chapter as well as in the following one, we shall confine our attention to cases of two alternatives. In Chapter Four, we shall proceed to cases of more than two alternatives.

2. Social Decision Function and Logical Function. In an issue composed of only two alternatives (x, y), a social decision R or an individual decision R_j is reduced to a three-valued variable D or D_j, respectively. D takes on three values xPy, xIy, yPx and D_j takes on three values xP_jy, xI_jy, yP_jx. Moreover, for any given ordered pair of alternatives (x, y), xP_jy, xI_jy, yP_jx may be expressed simply as $1, 0, -1$, which may be dubbed, respectively, *pro*, abstention and *con*, concerning the issue x against y. Similarly, $1, 0, -1$ may stand for xPy, xIy, yPx.

Thus, in a world of two alternatives, any social

decision function can be expressed as a function of the form:

$$D = F(D_1, D_2, \ldots, D_n)$$

The domain of the function is now the n-fold Cartesian product of the set $\{1, 0, -1\}$ and its range is the set $\{1, 0, -1\}$. In this class of functions, every combination of three-valued variables specifies a three-valued variable. We are going to show that this particular type of function is identical with *truth function* in *three-valued logic*.

The concept of *truth function* is one of the most fundamental concepts in symbolic logic. A full elucidation of this basic concept is beyond the scope of this book; the reader may refer, for example, to J. A. Faris' book.[1] For the present purpose, however, we may roughly define a truth function in its elementary form as a rule according to which every combination of variables taking the value of 'true' or 'false' specifies a variable taking the value of true or false. In other words, this function is formally equivalent to a function whose domain is the multi-fold Cartesian product of the set $\{1, 0\}$ and whose range is the set $\{1, 0\}$. A truth function is initially defined in a setting of *two-valued logic*.

Two-valued logic can naturally be extended to *three-valued logic*, where every variable takes on three values $1, 0, -1$. For example, in so-called modal logic, every variable takes on three values; 'necessarily true', 'probably true' or 'false'. For another example, our social decision function in a world of two alternatives can be regarded as a three-valued truth function,

[1] Faris, J. A.: *Truth-Functional Logic*, Ch. 2.

where three values are 'x is preferred to y', 'x is indifferent to y' and 'y is preferred to x'.

Various problems in two-valued logic can similarly be posed and solved in three-valued logic. Specifically, let us here tackle a so-called 'technical completeness problem'. In two-valued logic, technical completeness problem asks if an arbitrary logical function can be expressed by only a few logical operators, such as $\sim$ and v, $\sim$ and . , or $\sim$ and $\supset$. In fact, it has long been established that any one of the above pairs of operators—negation and disjunction, negation and conjunction or negation and implication—is capable of expressing any truth function in two-valued logic.

The same problem in many-valued logic is more difficult to tackle, but Rosser and Turquette have successfully solved it. Let us introduce their conclusion in terms of three-valued logic.

Rosser and Turquette's Theorem: Any three-valued truth function can be expressed by the three logical operators, Łukasiewicz-Tarski's **C** operator, Łukasiewicz-Tarski's **N** operator and Słupecki's **T** operator.

In the following argument, we shall use capital letters X, X_1, X_2, . . . to represent logical variables. If a three-valued logical variable is thought of as taking on the values 1, 0, -1, the logical operators mentioned above may be defined as follows:

Łukasiewicz-Tarski's **C** operator is a two-place predicate such that $\mathbf{C}(X_1, X_2)$ takes on the value of min $(1, X_2 - X_1 + 1)$.
Łukasiewicz-Tarski's **N** operator is a one-place predicate such that $\mathbf{N}(X)$ takes on the value of $-X$.

18

Slupecki's **T** operator is a one-place predicate such that **T**(X) takes on the constant value 0.

The **C** operator is one—among several—of the extensions of implication operator in two-valued logic. The **N** operator is a three-valued version of negation operator. On the other hand, the **T** operator has no counterpart in two-valued logic. As in two-valued logic, any three-valued logical function—therefore, any social decision function—can be expressed by a few logical operators. We now proceed to modify the theorem so that we can apply it to the analysis of social decisions.

3. Voting Operator. We have already mentioned *voting* as a typical rule of social decision-making. As one of the social decision functions, voting can also be regarded as a three-valued logical function.

Definition (voting): A three-valued logical function $F(X_1, X_2, \ldots, X_m)$ is called a *voting operator* or, more simply, a *voting*, if the function takes on the values 1, 0, −1, accordingly as $X_1 + X_2 + \ldots + X_m$ is positive, zero or negative.

A voting operator $F(X_1, X_2, \ldots, X_m)$ is, in this book, denoted by the symbol:

$$((X_1, X_2, \ldots, X_m))$$

If 1, 0, −1 are regarded as *pro*, abstention and *con* respectively, this logical operator can be interpreted exactly as a familiar social decision-making rule called *voting procedure*.

It must here be noted that the voting of our definition is an operator which can be used as freely as the rules of predicate logic allow. For example, a result of voting itself may enter another voting operator like:

$$((\,((X_1,\ X_2,\ X_1)),\ X_3,\ ((X_2,\ X_4,\ X_5))\,))$$

Moreover, the same variable, such as X_1 in the above example, may enter a voting more than once, or the same variable, such as X_2, may enter more than one voting.

Most familiar is the case where each variable appears only once under one voting operator. In terms of social decision functions, such function may be called a *simple majority voting* or, more literally, a *direct democracy*.

Definition (simple majority voting): A social decision function $F(D_1,\ D_2, \ldots,\ D_n)$ is called a *simple majority voting* or a *direct democracy*, if:

$$F(D_1,\ D_2, \ldots,\ D_n) \equiv ((D_1,\ D_2, \ldots,\ D_n))$$

A direct democracy is obviously the simplest example of the social decision functions composed of voting procedures. An immediate extension is probably an *indirect democracy* or a *representative system*, where several voting operators are combined. Beside these typical examples, we can find many other examples of social decision functions. The next section will try to investigate the structures of various social decision functions in terms of voting operator.

4. Expression in Terms of Voting. Let us now note that the **C** operator $C(X_1,\ X_2)$ is equivalent to $((-X_1,\ X_2,\ 1))$, and the **T** operator $T(X)$ is equivalent to $((X,\ -X))$. The **N** operator $N(X)$ may be denoted simply by $-X$. Then Rosser and Turquette's theorem can be transformed into:

Social Decision Function

Theorem 2–1: Any three-valued truth-function (or a social decision function) can be expressed by votings, negations and constants such as 1, 0, −1.

Any rule of social decision-making can be expressed by voting procedures mixed with negations and constants.

Let us explain this theorem by several actual examples. At one extreme of social decision functions, there is the rule of *jury decision*, by which we mean such a rule that only a unanimous preference by all the individuals results in a social decision, and otherwise social indifference ensues. For convenience of exposition, let us suppose that the number of individuals is three. Then a social decision function representing the rule of jury decision is expressed as:

$$((((D_1, D_1, D^*)), ((D_2, D_2, D^*)), ((D_3, D_3, D^*)),$$
$$((-D_1, -D_2, -D_3))))$$

where D^* is short for $((-D_1, -D_2, -D_3, ((D_1, D_2, D_3))))$. In order to verify this equivalence, we have to construct a truth table in three-valued logic. For example, D^* has the following table:

D_1	D_2	D_3	D^*	D_1	D_2	D_3	D^*	D_1	D_2	D_3	D^*
1	1	1	−1	0	1	1	−1	−1	1	1	0
1	1	0	−1	0	1	0	0	−1	1	0	0
1	1	−1	0	0	1	−1	0	−1	1	−1	0
1	0	1	−1	0	0	1	0	−1	0	1	0
1	0	0	0	0	0	0	0	−1	0	0	0
1	0	−1	0	0	0	−1	0	−1	0	−1	1
1	−1	1	0	0	−1	1	0	−1	−1	1	0
1	−1	0	0	0	−1	0	0	−1	−1	0	1
1	−1	−1	0	0	−1	−1	1	−1	−1	−1	1

By constructing the truth table, we can similarly verify that the above function as a whole is equal to

21

1 if $D_1 = D_2 = D_3 = 1$, is equal to -1 if $D_1 = D_2 = D_3 = -1$, and is equal to 0 in any other cases. The function is expressed by votings and negations.

Similarly, we may consider *two-thirds majority voting*, which has, in fact, several versions. One of those versions in a society of six individuals can be expressed as:

$$((\,((D_1,\ D_2,\ D_3,\ D_4,\ D_5,\ D_6,\ -1,\ -1)),$$
$$((D_1,\ D_2,\ D_3,\ D_4,\ D_5,\ D_6,\ -1,\ -1)),\ 1))$$

An alternative in question, say, x can be preferred to y the contrary alternative, only when no less than two-thirds of those individuals who do not abstain prefer x to y. For example, the general assembly of the United Nations adopts this rule regarding an issue specified as important, such as the admittance of the People's Republic of China.

Sometimes, a committee stipulates a *quorum*, which means that the committee's decision is indifference, if the abstaining ballots are more than a predetermined number. For example, the rule of *one-half quorum* requires that more than one-half of the individuals avoid abstention. This rule in a society of three individuals can also be expressed by votings and negations:

$$((\,((D_1,\ D_2,\ D_3)),$$
$$((\,((D_1,\ D_1,\ ((-D_2,\ -D_3))\,))),$$
$$((D_2,\ D_2,\ ((-D_1,\ -D_3))\,))),$$
$$((D_3,\ D_3,\ ((-D_1,\ -D_2))\,)))\,))\,))$$

The truth table will verify that the society fails to support any alternative if more than one individual abstain, and that otherwise the rule is equivalent to $((D_1, D_2, D_3))$.

22

To a *dictatorship*, there corresponds a social decision function of the form

$$((D_1, D_1, D_1, D_2, D_3))$$

which is equivalent to D_1, if $D_1 \neq 0$ and equivalent to $((D_2, D_3))$, if $D_1 = 0$.

A *traditional society* may be expressed as

$$((D_1, D_2, 1, 1, 1))$$

where 1 represents the fixed decision which supports a certain alternative.

All social decision functions can in a similar way be expressed by means of votings, negations and constants. It must be noted that an expression of a given social decision function may not be unique. For example, the simplest social decision function $((D_1, D_2))$ is equivalent to a more complicated form:

$$((D_1, D_1, ((1, D_2)), D_2, ((-1, D_2)))).$$

5. Decisive Group. As the above examples suggest, there are various types of social decision functions. In the rule of jury decision, the agreement of all individual decisions is necessary for arriving at a social choice. In the case of two-thirds majority voting, the agreement among two-thirds of the individuals is required. Most typically, a social choice under simple majority voting needs the support of more than half of all the individuals. We may conceive one-third minority voting on an issue x against y, which is equivalent to two-thirds majority voting on an issue y against x. In this case, only more than one-third of all individuals is needed to arrive at a social choice of x. Lastly, if a society is dictatorial, a certain individual's choice becomes a social choice.

We may now introduce the concept of *decisive group*. If a group of individuals is so powerful that their coalition always dominates the society, the group is called a decisive group. More exactly:

Definition (decisive group): With respect to a given social decision function, a group of individuals is called *decisive* for an issue x against y, if, whenever each member of the group prefers x to y, the society does likewise regardless of other individuals' decisions.

For example, in a society of three individuals where simple majority voting is adopted, any group composed of more than one individual is decisive for *any* issue of two alternatives. Generally speaking, however, a decisive group for an issue x against y may not be decisive for the reversed issue y against x. The two-thirds majority voting introduced in the last section is a typical example. In the example of the general assembly of the United Nations, a group of one-third of the member nations is decisive for the issue, rejection of the People's Republic of China versus its acceptance, whereas a group of two-thirds of the member nations is decisive for the issue, acceptance against rejection.

With respect to a given social decision function, there are usually many decisive groups. Among them we shall pay particular attention to the smallest decisive group.

Definition (minimal decisive group): A decisive group for an issue x against y is called *minimal*, if any smaller group included in the group in question is not decisive for the issue.

A minimal decisive group is a group of those individuals, each of whom is essential to the group's dominant position. In the example of simply majority voting of the form

$$((D_1, D_2, D_3))$$

any group of two individuals—that is, $\{1, 2\}$, $\{1, 3\}$, $\{2, 3\}$—is a minimal decisive group. It is to be noted that generally a minimal decisive group may be of different sizes as in the following social decision function

$$((D_1, ((D_2, D_3, D_4)), ((D_5, D_6, D_7, D_8, D_9))))$$

where the groups $\{1, 2, 3\}$, $\{1, 5, 6, 7\}$ and $\{2, 3, 5, 6, 7\}$ are all minimally decisive.

6. Types of Domination. A minimal decisive group may be of any size. In some cases, it may coincide with the group of all the individuals. It may be a group made up of more than one-half of all individuals. It may be one particular individual. Sometimes it may even be empty.

The size of a minimal decisive group may be useful as an index of the degree of domination in a society. If a minimal decisive group is small, in comparison with the group of all individuals, then we may say that domination by the decisive group is comparatively strong. If a minimal decisive group is comparatively large, domination by the decisive group is said to be weak. The size of a minimal decisive group may be thought of as an inversely related index of the degree of domination.

An example of the weakest type of domination is the rule of jury decision. A jury decision can be reached only if all jurors agree; the minimal decisive group is, in this case, the group of all individuals. The rule of two-thirds majority voting is stronger in domination than the rule of jury decision but is weaker than simple majority voting. In the case of simple majority voting, the number of individuals in the minimal decisive groups is the smallest integer greater than one-half of the number of all individuals.

In ordinary representative systems, the degree of domination is stronger than in simple majority voting. The size of minimal decisive groups is less than one-half of all individuals. For example, in a representative system like

$$((\,((D_1,\ D_2,\ D_3)),\ ((D_4,\ D_5,\ D_6)),\ ((D_7,\ D_8,\ D_9))\,))$$

minimal decisive groups consist of four individuals, so is a minority.

At the extreme, if a minimal decisive group consists of only one individual, the degree of domination becomes maximal. If a particular individual is decisive for the issue x against y as well as the issue y against x, the minimal decisive group is unique, so that this individual deserves the name of *dictator*.

To the extent that a non-empty minimal decisive group exists, the degree of domination ranges from the jury decision to the dictatorial rule. Most social decision functions are logically situated somewhere between the above two extremes, according to their degrees of domination. In fact, we can prove:

Theorem 2–2: With respect to a social decision function $F(D_1, D_2, \ldots, D_n)$ on an issue x against y, there exists a minimal decisive group for the issue x against y, if and only if unanimity rule of preference holds or, more symbolically, if and only if:

$$F(1, 1, \ldots, 1) = 1$$

Proof: (sufficiency) If $F(1, 1, \ldots, 1) = 1$, or if unanimity rule of preference holds, then a group of all individuals is decisive so that an existence of a minimal decisive group is obvious, though a minimal decisive group may possibly be empty.

(necessity) Suppose that unanimity rule of preference does not hold or, more symbolically, $F(1, 1, \ldots, 1) = 0$ or -1. Further suppose that there exists a decisive group; if $D_j = 1$ for all j in that group, then $D = 1$ irrespective of other individuals' decisions. However, consider the case where $D_j = 1$ for all individuals. Then, by supposition, $D = 0$ or -1. This contradicts the decisiveness of the group. *Q.E.D.*

We shall later find out that the *unanimity rule of preference* is one of the important properties of social decision functions. In fact, we shall show in Chapter Six that social decision functions can be classified into two categories: the unanimity rule of preference holds in the first category, while the *anti-unanimity rule of preference*—which means $F(1, 1, \ldots, 1) = -1$ —holds in the second. So far as the first category is concerned, social decision functions can be arranged on the spectrum of domination. Between two extremes of jury decision and dictatorship, there are many intermediary cases on the spectrum, among which we shall turn, in the next chapter, to a familiar class of social decision-making rule called a *democracy*.

Suggested Reading

Faris, J. A.: *Truth-Functional Logic* (1962)
Rosser, J. B. and A. R. Turquette: *Many-Valued Logic* (1952)

Chapter Three

DEMOCRACY IN A WORLD
OF TWO ALTERNATIVES

1. Definition of Democracy. Within the spectrum of social decision functions, this chapter is concerned with the particular social decision-making rule called *democracy*. The definition of democracy is one of the most controversial matters in the field of the social sciences, so that even an introduction to the topic could form the subject of a substantial book. This little book must, therefore, neglect all the historical background underlying the concept and practice of democracy, and start by simply defining it. Let us agree, then, with Lord Bryce in his *Modern Democracies* that

'. . . democracy really means nothing more nor less than the rule of the whole people expressing their sovereign will by their votes.'

In other words, we define a *democracy* as a social decision function *consisting of and only of voting procedures*. In the light of Theorem 2–1, our definition may be given as follows:

Definition (democracy): A social decision function $F(D_1, D_2, \ldots, D_n)$ is called a *democracy*, if the function can be expressed only by voting operators —without any resort to negations and constants— and the function is nondictatorial,

where nondictatorship is defined as follows:

Definition (nondictatorship): A social decision function $F(D_1, D_2, \ldots, D_n)$ is called *nondictatorial*, if there is no individual whose preference is always adopted by the society:

$$\sim(\exists j)[(D_j \neq 0) \supset \{D_j = F(D_1, D_2, \ldots, D_n)\}]$$

Let us note here that, if a social decision is always an indifference, then the social decision function is not a democracy; in fact, such a function cannot be expressed as a compound of and only of voting operators— without resort to negations or logical constants such as 0.

In verbal terms, a democracy is a hierarchy of voting procedures each of which may be called a *committee*. Each individual casts a ballot or ballots in some committee or committees. The decisions of the committees are represented in a higher committee whose decisions are, in turn, represented in a still higher committee and so on. Finally, the society's decision will be reached in the supreme committee. By virtue of the nondictatorship condition, there is no dictatorial individual in the supreme committee.

A typical example is *simple majority voting*. Equally typical is a so to speak 'perfect representative system' such as:

$$((\,((D_1, D_2, D_3)),\ ((D_4, D_5, D_6)),\ ((D_7, D_8, D_9))\,))$$

The supreme committee is composed of three representatives, each of which stands for the decision of a committee of three individuals. However, most of the examples of democracy in our definition are not so simple. All in all, the above definition is a description of 'democracy' in its widest sense, so that every conceivable combination of voting procedures is permitted within this definition.

Let us note here that an apparently nondemocratic social decision function may possibly be democratic. For example:

$$((D_1, D_2, D_3)) = -((-D_1, -D_2, -D_3))$$

The right-hand term includes negations but, in fact, those negations are not indispensable. Usually, an equivalence is not so obvious. For example:

$$((D_1, D_2, D_3)) = ((D_1, D_1, ((1, D_2, D_3)), \\ ((D_2, D_3)), ((-1, D_2, D_3))))$$

We can verify an equivalence by constructing a truth table; the constants $1, -1$ are inessential. Similarly, the negation in the following example can be dispensed with:

$$((D_1, D_2, D_3)) = ((D_1, D_1, ((D_1, D_2, D_3)), \\ ((D_2, D_3)), ((-D_1, D_2, D_3))))$$

We regard these social decision functions as *democratic*, because in practice they cannot be distinguished from the corresponding democratic social decision functions.

It is to be remembered that we are considering only the issues consisting of two alternatives. We now proceed to discover, in this world of two alternatives, a logical condition for democracy or, in the light of Theorem 2–1, a condition for the exclusion of negations and constants. In the next section, we shall be concerned with eliminating the constants.

2. Self-duality. In terms of a theory of decision-making, a logical constant can be regarded as a fixed decision on an issue in question. In any democratic system, a social decision should be influenced by and only by the people's will. Thus we may impose the condition of *autonomy* as a prerequisite of democracy.

> *Definition* (autonomy): A social decision function is called *autonomous*, if no fixed ballot representing an outside decision enters any voting, or, more formally, if the function can be expressed by voting operators and negations, without resort to constants.

We are going to present a necessary and sufficient condition for *autonomy*.

Let us now formulate a concept of *duality* in three-valued logic. In ordinary two-valued logic, the dual of a truth function is defined by a negation of each variable, and a negation of the function as a whole. Keeping the analogy, we can define duality in three-valued logic as follows:

> *Definition* (duality): A truth function $-F(-X_1, -X_2, \ldots, -X_m)$ is called the dual of a function $F(X_1, X_2, \ldots, X_m)$.

Then we can define self-duality as follows:

> *Definition* (self-duality): A logical function is called *self-dual*, if the primal and the dual are equivalent:

$$F(-X_1, -X_2, \ldots, -X_m) \equiv -F(X_1, X_2, \ldots, X_m)$$

In terms of social decision functions, this means that if every individual decision is reversed, then a social decision is also reversed. K. O. May called this pro-

31

perty *neutrality*. This book reserves this term for another property which we shall consider later.

First we can readily assert:

Theorem 3–1: A voting procedure involving no logical constants is self-dual:

$$-((D_1, D_2, \ldots, D_m)) \equiv ((-D_1, -D_2, \ldots, -D_m))$$

Then we can establish:

Theorem 3–2: A social decision function is autonomous, if and only if the function is self-dual.

Proof: (necessity) By Theorem 3–1, a negation operation in front of a voting operator involving no constants can be brought within that voting operator. Suppose that a social decision function is autonomous, so that it can be expressed by votings and negations, without resort to constants. Starting with a negation operation in front of the function, repeat the bringing-in process. Finally, we can arrive at self-duality.

(sufficiency) Suppose that a social decision function is self-dual. By Theorem 2–1, this function can be expressed by votings, negations and logical constants. Then, consider a derived function F^* such that a constant 1 in F is replaced by

$$((D_1, D_1, ((D_2, D_2, ((D_3, \ldots \atop ((D_{n-1}, D_{n-1}, D_n)) \ldots))))))$$

and a constant -1 in F is replaced by its negation. Note that F^* involves no constants, so that it is self-dual.

If $D_1 = 1$, evidently:

$$F(1, D_2, \ldots, D_n) \equiv F^*(1, D_2, \ldots, D_n)$$

Democracy in a World of Two Alternatives

By self-duality of F and F^*:

$$F(-1, -D_2, \ldots, -D_n) \equiv F^*(-1, -D_2, \ldots, -D_n)$$

which can be written without any loss of generality as:

$$F(-1, D_2, \ldots, D_n) \equiv F^*(-1, D_2, \ldots, D_n)$$

Then, if $D_1 = 0$ and $D_2 = 1$, evidently:

$$F(0, 1, D_3, \ldots, D_n) \equiv F^*(0, 1, D_3, \ldots, D_n)$$

As before, we have:

$$F(0, -1, D_3, \ldots, D_n) \equiv F^*(0, -1, D_3, \ldots, D_n)$$

By repeating this process, we can establish that, for all combinations of $D_1, D_2, \ldots, D_n$ except the case where all D_js are equal to zero, $F = F^*$.

If all D_js are equal to zero, then $F(0, 0, \ldots, 0) = -F(0, 0, \ldots, 0)$ by self-duality so that $F(0, 0, \ldots, 0) = 0$. Evidently, $F^*(0, 0, \ldots, 0) = 0$. Thus, for all combinations of $D_1, D_2, \ldots, D_n$, $F \equiv F^*$. Q.E.D.

3. Meaning of Self-duality. As long as we are considering the world of two alternatives, self-duality can be regarded as impartiality or neutrality with respect to alternatives. A self-dual social decision function has exactly the same structure regarding issue x against y as it does regarding issue y against x. Any *autonomous* society—therefore, any *democratic* society—is required to treat alternatives in an impartial or neutral manner.

Let us now examine one example of two-thirds majority voting:

$$((D_1, D_2, D_3, D_4, D_5, -1, -1))$$

where self-duality is obviously violated. The society's

pro on the issue in question requires a two-thirds majority, while the society's *con* requires only the objection of more than one-third of all individuals. This two-thirds majority voting is not impartial with respect to alternatives.

Some societies actually adopt a rule of two-thirds majority voting, when a fundamental change in the existing state of affairs is pitted against the existing state. An amendment of the Japanese Constitution requires the agreement of two-thirds of all members of the Diet. In any rigid-type constitution like this example, the existing state of affairs is given a favourable bias.

This situation can be generalized. If a society adopts a rule of three-fourths majority voting on an issue x against y, this amounts to adopting a rule of one-fourth 'minority' voting on an issue y against x. More generally, we can assert:

Theorem 3–3: Any majority voting rule other than a simple one-half is not self-dual, so not autonomous.

The larger the size of the majority required to arrive at a particular alternative, say, the new state of affairs, the smaller will be the likelihood of the society's deciding to abandon, say, the existing state of the society. The greater the size of the required majority, the greater will be the influence of a minority group.

If a constant representing a fixed decision on an issue enters some committee in a society, then the committee adopts some majority voting rule other than one-half majority so that, in fact, some minority rule prevails there. If a democracy is to rest on the principle of majority voting, then one-half majority voting is the only admissible form. Thus, self-duality may justifiably be regarded as a prerequisite of democracy.

4. Monotonicity. In this section, we shall try to discover a condition for an absence of negations in logical functions. As we mentioned before, a democracy in our definition is a hierarchy of committees; each committee's decision is represented in a higher committee whose decision is, in its turn, represented in a still higher committee and so on. In other words, our democracy is a *representative system* in the widest sense. We now require that in any representative system, a representative should faithfully stand for the decision of the committee which he represents, and that when an individual casts his ballots, his decision should be faithfully expressed. Thus, as a second prerequisite for democracy, we impose the condition of *faithful representation*.

> *Definition* (faithful representation): A social decision function is said to satisfy the condition of *faithful representation*, if any decisions reached by individuals or voting procedures are always faithfully represented in the process of social decision-making, or, more formally, if the function can be expressed by voting operators and constants, without resort to negations.

Our aim in this section is to discover a condition for faithful representation.

Let us now introduce a logical concept.

> *Definition* (strong monotonicity): A logical function $F(X_1, X_2, \ldots, X_m)$ is called *strongly monotonic*, if the following two conditions hold:

35

(1) If $F(X_1, X_2, \ldots, X_m) = 0$ or 1, $X'_j = X_j$ for all $j \neq j_0$, and $X'_{j_0} > X_{j_0}$, then $F(X'_1, X'_2, \ldots, X'_m) = 1$.

(2) If $F(X_1, X_2, \ldots, X_m) = 0$ or -1, $X'_j = X_j$ for all $j \neq j_0$, and $X'_{j_0} < X_{j_0}$, then $F(X'_1, X'_2, \ldots, X'_m) = -1$.

In terms of social decision problems, if some individual changes his decision in favour of an alternative x against y, then the society also changes its decision in favour of x or, if the society already prefers x to y, it maintains its preference. The point of this *strong* monotonicity is that any and every individual can break a social indecision. K. O. May's *positive responsiveness* condition only requires condition (1) in the above definition. Under self-duality, condition (1) implies condition (2) and *vice versa*, so that May's condition is equivalent to ours under self-duality.

We can now establish:

Theorem 3–4: A social decision function satisfies the condition of faithful representation, if the function is strongly monotonic.

Proof: By constructing a truth table, it can easily be verified that, for any strongly monotonic function F:

$$F(D_1, D_2, \ldots, D_n) \equiv ((F(1, D_2, \ldots, D_n), F(0, D_2, \ldots, D_n), F(-1, D_2, \ldots, D_n), D_1, D_1))$$

The three $(n-1)$-argumented functions in the above voting operator are also strongly monotonic. Therefore, each of three $(n-1)$-argumented functions can also be expressed by a voting whose five entries are occupied by three $(n-2)$-argumented functions and

36

two D_2s. By repeating this process, we can finally bring out all the variables from the original function and construct a structure of voting operators without any help from negations. *Q.E.D.*

However, the converse is not true. For example, let us consider a function

$$((((D_1, D_2, D_3)), ((D_4, D_5, D_6))))$$

and suppose that $D_1 = D_2 = D_3 = -1$ and $D_4 = D_5 = D_6 = 1$, so that the function is equal to zero. Then suppose that D_1 changes to 1 but the function remains equal to zero. This gives a counter-example against the statement that faithful representation implies strong monotonicity. This property is, in fact, characteristic of a representative system. In a direct democracy, every individual has the power to break a social indifference. But, in a representative system, an individual can cast a decisive vote only under rare circumstances. Even if the Conservatives and the Socialists happened to be equal in number in the House of Commons in all probability no individual voter nor any small group of individual voters could break the balance, because every elected candidate would probably win by a considerable margin over his opponent. Strong monotonicity is sufficient, but not necessary for faithful representation or for the absence of negations in a social decision function.

Thus let us try a weaker concept which may be called a *weak monotonicity* or, more simply, *monotonicity*.

Definition (monotonicity): A function $F(X_1, X_2, \ldots, X_m)$ is called *monotonic*, if

$$(j)(X'_j \geqq X_j) \supset (F(X'_1, X'_2, \ldots, X'_m) \geqq F(X_1, X_2, \ldots, X_m))$$

37

In other words, if every individual's decision remains the same or changes in favour of an alternative x, then a social decision also remains the same or changes in favour of x. Under monotonicity a social decision is allowed to remain the same, in spite of the change of some individual's decision. K. J. Arrow's condition of *positive association* is closely related to this condition. J. H. Blau's 'monotonicity' condition is even closer. We shall later investigate the logical relations among those closely related concepts. Now we can assert:

> *Theorem* 3–5: A social decision function satisfies the condition of faithful representation, only if the function is monotonic.

If a social decision function is expressed only by votings and constants, then by the nature of voting operators the function is monotonic.

However, the converse is again false. Let us consider an artificial example.

$$((\,((D_1,\ D_1,\ ((-D_3,\ 1))\,)),\ ((D_2,\ D_2,\ -D_3)),$$
$$((D_1,\ D_1,\ ((-D_3,\ -1))\,)),\ D_3,\ D_3))$$

A truth table of this function is as follows:

D_1	D_2	D_3	D	D_1	D_2	D_3	D	D_1	D_2	D_3	D
1	1	1	1	0	1	1	1	-1	1	1	1
1	1	0	1	0	1	0	1	-1	1	0	-1
1	1	-1	1	0	1	-1	0	-1	1	-1	-1
1	0	1	1	0	0	1	0	-1	0	1	-1
1	0	0	1	0	0	0	0	-1	0	0	-1
1	0	-1	1	0	0	-1	0	-1	0	-1	-1
1	-1	1	1	0	-1	1	0	-1	-1	1	-1
1	-1	0	1	0	-1	0	-1	-1	-1	0	-1
1	-1	-1	-1	0	-1	-1	-1	-1	-1	-1	-1

Evidently, the function is monotonic as well as self-dual. None of the three variables can be removed from

38

the function, because any one of them affects the value of the function. We are now going to show that this function cannot be expressed by votings and constants, without resort to negations. Consider a case where $D_1 = D_2 = 0$ and $D_3 = 1$, so that $F = 0$. If the function could be expressed without resort to negations, $D_3 = 1$ could be cancelled only by a constant -1. The existence of -1 means, however, that $D_1 = D_2 = D_3 = 0$ must imply $F = -1$. But this contradicts $F = 0$. Therefore, this function cannot be expressed without the help of negation operators. Monotonicity cannot be sufficient for the absence of negations.

Now we have a logical inequality relation. A necessary and sufficient condition for faithful representation is weaker than *strong monotonicity* and stronger than *monotonicity*. Our problem is to give a proper logical expression to this logical entity. The author's tentative conclusion is that there is no meaningful expression from the present standpoint.

5. Monotonicity under Resoluteness. In the last section, we have left unfinished the task of presenting a necessary and sufficient condition for the absence of negation operators. Thus, this section imposes certain restrictions, under which a necessary and sufficient condition for faithful representation will be given.

First we may note that monotonicity and strong monotonicity differ only if a social indifference occurs. When a social indifference is forbidden, the two kinds of monotonicity will coincide, so that a necessary and sufficient condition for faithful representation will be monotonicity or, equivalently, strong monotonicity. We shall examine this idea more carefully. For this purpose, the following two cases may be distinguished; (1) individual indifference and social indifference are both forbidden, and (2) individual indifference is permitted, but social indifference is forbidden.

Let us begin with case (1). In this case, individual decision and social decision both take one of the two values 1, −1. A social decision function is now regarded as a two-valued logical function. As in the three-valued case, any logical function in two-valued logic can be expressed by votings, negations and logical constants, where every voting has an odd number of entries. Then recalling that monotonicity and strong monotonicity cannot be distinguished in two-valued logic, we can prove:

Theorem 3–6: If an indifference (individual and social) is forbidden, then (i) a necessary and sufficient condition for autonomy is self-duality; and (ii) a necessary and sufficient condition for faithful representation is monotonicity.

The proof which is similar to, and much easier than, the proof in the three-valued case, is left to the reader.

Case (2) requires more careful investigations. Any social decision-making rule which never induces a social indifference constitutes a particular type of social decision function, whose range as a function is restricted. We may call this class *resolute*. Then we can immediately assert:

Theorem 3–7: A resolute social decision function satisfies the condition of faithful representation, if and only if the function is monotonic, or, equivalently in this case, strongly monotonic.

This formally correct statement is, however, not very interesting since *resoluteness* is inconsistent with self-duality, another prerequisite for democracy. For, if all individuals abstain, a social indifference cannot be avoided without resort to some outside decisions, that is, the introduction of constants.

Resoluteness may be too restrictive to be practical. We may conceive weaker versions of 'resolute' social decision functions. In actual examples of the democratic system, devices are built into a social decision-making rule to avoid a social indifference. For example, a chairman can cast his vote only when a tie occurs in a committee over which he presides (e.g. the Vice-president in the U.S. Senate). This decision-making rule may be expressed as

$$((D_1, D_1, D_2, D_2, \ldots, D_n, D_n, D_{n+1}))$$

where D_{n+1} signifies the chairman's decision. The reader may verify that monotonicity and strong monotonicity are equivalent in this particular social decision function, even if a social indifference sometimes occurs.

This 'chairman's rule' may be generalized as follows:

Definition (quasi-resoluteness): A social decision function is called *quasi-resolute*, if a social indifference results only when all of the individuals belonging to a given group abstain.

'A given group' in the definition may be interpreted as a group of chairmen of various committees. In particular, if 'a given group' coincides with the whole society or, in other words, if a social indifference occurs only when all individuals are indifferent, then

41

evidently monotonicity implies strong monotonicity so that monotonicity is sufficient for faithful representation. However, quasi-resoluteness is, generally speaking, not always sufficient for the equivalence between monotonicity and strong monotonicity. We shall refer to this concept later.

Lastly, let us present a practical, though less elegant, theorem. In many actual rules of social decision-making, little attention has been paid to preventing social indifferences which might be harmful if they really occurred. The main reason for this laxity is probably that a social indifference is ordinarily unlikely. Sharing the same laxity, we shall observe only those cases where the society does not abstain. More formally, for any decision function F, let us consider an auxiliary function F^* such that, whenever $F = 0$ and $D_j \neq 0$ for some j, F^* is undefined, and otherwise $F^* = F$. Then, for this social decision function whose domain as well as range is limited, we have:

> *Theorem* 3–8: A function F^* can be expressed by votings and constants without resort to any negation operators, if and only if the function F is monotonic.

In so far as we can omit the cases of social indifference, a monotonic social decision function satisfies a condition of *faithful representation*. For instance, for the counter-example shown after Theorem 3–5, the following auxiliary function can be substituted:

$$((((((D_1, D_2)), ((D_1, D_3)), ((D_2, D_3))))),$$
$$(((((D_1, D_2)), ((D_1, D_3)), ((D_2, D_3))))), D_1))$$

In so far as no social indifference occurs, this auxiliary function is equivalent to the counter-example; we can express the former function without negations, while we cannot express the latter without them.

6. Monotonicity under Single Entry. In the last section, resoluteness or similar restrictions helped us to derive a necessary and sufficient condition for faithful representation. In this section, we shall discover other restrictions which can play the same role. We must ask, above all, if the other prerequisites for democracy, i.e. self-duality and nondictatorship, are helpful. However, the counter-example shown after Theorem 3–5 gives a negative answer. In that example, a social function was monotonic, as well as self-dual and non-dictatorial, but could not dispense with negations. Self-duality and nondictatorship are independent of the condition for faithful representation.

In our definition, democracy is a very broad concept; an individual may join more than one committee or may even cast more than one vote. We might strengthen our requirement so that every individual can join only one committee. Or, more formally, it might be required that a social decision function be expressed by voting operators, negations and constants in such a way that each individual variable can enter only one voting operator. This additional requirement will be called the *single entry condition*.

Under this condition, we can assert:

Theorem 3–9: Suppose that every individual can join only one committee. A social decision function satisfies the condition of faithful representation, if and only if the function is monotonic.

Proof: Suppose that a social decision function is expressed by votings, logical constants and negations.

By the same reasoning shown in Theorems 3–1 and 3–2, any negation operators can be brought into the positions which directly qualify individual ballots and constants. For example:

$$-((((D_1, 1)), D_2, -((D_3, D_4, -1))))$$
$$= (((((-D_1, -1)), -D_2, ((D_3, D_4, -1))))$$

Corresponding to any social decision function, we can always construct a canonical form such that negation operators qualify D_js but not voting operators.

By our supposition, a canonical form of the function involves some individual ballot qualified by a negation, that is, it involves $-D_j$. Then suppose that $D_j = 0$. By single entry condition, we can always find a combination of individual ballots such that the value of every voting operator in the canonical form—including the canonical form itself—is equal to 0. (If the function takes on a constant value, then the function is trivially monotonic and can be expressed only by a constant.) In the example shown above, a required combination is $D_1 = -1, D_2 = 0, D_3 = 0$ and $D_4 = 1$. Then suppose that $D_j = 1$, without any change in the values of all other individual ballots. The value of the function is now equal to -1 because D_j enters only as $-D_j$. This contradicts monotonicity. *Q.E.D.*

The proof suggests that our trouble is due to an interdependence between the committees in the society. Our single entry condition removes this interdependence so that monotonicity becomes not only necessary but also sufficient for the absence of negation operators. As a simple corollary which is perhaps worth presenting, we can establish:

Theorem 3–10: Suppose that every individual can

cast only one vote. Then a social decision function satisfies the condition of faithful representation if and only if the function is monotonic.

A condition of single entry as in Theorem 3–9, or a condition of single vote, as in Theorem 3–10, is not at all unusual. They may even be regarded as additional prerequisites for democracy. We may say that monotonicity is, in many standard cases of democratic system, a necessary and sufficient condition for faithful representation.

7. Conditions for Democracy. Let us now summarize the argument in this chapter. If we combine, first of all, Theorem 3–2 and Theorem 3–5, we can assert:

Theorem 3–11: A social decision function is a democracy, only if the function is self-dual, monotonic and nondictatorial.

It must be noted that self-duality, monotonicity and nondictatorship are mutually independent, as shown by the example following Theorem 3–5. A necessary condition for democracy has now been given.

In this book, we shall mainly be concerned with necessary conditions for democracy—and their possible inconsistency—rather than with the sufficient conditions for democracy. However, a discovery of sufficient conditions is, no doubt, of theoretical interest. In connection with Theorem 3–11, we may be led to conjecture the following sufficient condition for democracy:

Conjectural theorem: A social decision function is a democracy, if the function is self-dual, strongly monotonic and nondictatorial.

One must note that Theorem 3–2 and Theorem 3–4 together cannot imply the above conjecture. A verification of this conjecture, in fact, requires a discouragingly lengthy argument. In this book, we had better leave the statement as a conjecture. An elegant proof of it is a challenge open to the reader.

However, it is useful to present some sufficient condition for democracy. As early as 1952, K. O. May presented a set of necessary and sufficient conditions for direct democracy or for simple majority voting. His theorem can be expressed in our terms as follows:

Theorem 3–12 (May's theorem): A social decision function is a direct democracy or a simple majority voting, if and only if the function is self-dual, strongly monotonic and symmetric.

where:

Definition (symmetry): A social decision function is called *symmetric*, if the function takes on the same value when two independent variables exchange their values:

$$F(D_1, \ldots, D_i, \ldots, D_j, \ldots, D_n)$$
$$= F(D_1, \ldots, D_j, \ldots, D_i, \ldots, D_n)$$
for all i, j $(i, j = 1, 2, \ldots, n)$.

Direct democracy, or simple majority voting, may be regarded as the strongest form of democracy. Any democratic system is thus located somewhere between the strongest condition given by May and the necessary condition shown in Theorem 3–11. May's condition is possibly the strongest sufficient condition for democracy.

We can conceive various types of democratic social decision functions. At one extreme, direct democracy is the strongest type of democracy. At the other extreme, democratic social decision functions can be only self-dual, monotonic and nondictatorial. For example, we may consider a typical representative system such as

$$((\ ((D_1,\ D_2,\ D_3)),\ ((D_4,\ D_5,\ D_6)),\ ((D_7,\ D_8,\ D_9))\ ))$$

We shall observe a remarkable difference in the degree of equality. The nondictatorship of our definition is the weakest form of egalitarian conditions in the sense that it prohibits the extreme form of inequality called dictatorship. On the other hand, the condition of symmetry is the strongest one; no more egalitarian condition can be conceived within the framework of social decision functions. The completely egalitarian condition in the form of symmetry is, indeed, a very strong condition. For example, the representative system introduced above is not symmetric. For let us consider a case

$$((\ ((1,\ 1,\ 1)),\ ((-1,\ 0,\ 1)),\ ((-1,\ -1,\ -1))\ ))$$

which is equal to 0. Then let us exchange D_3 and D_4. We now have

$$((\ ((1,\ 1,\ -1)),\ ((1,\ 0,\ 1)),\ ((-1,\ -1,\ -1))\ ))$$

which is equal to 1. This contradicts symmetry. In ordinary representative systems, individuals are not always 'equal'. In the above example, the fourth, fifth and sixth individuals are more influential than the rest of the individuals, because any change in the decision of any of these three individuals results in a

47

change in the social decision, while a change in any of the other individuals does not. No representative system can guarantee the complete equality which direct democracy can provide.

8. Several Examples. To conclude this chapter we shall consider whether various particular types of societies are democratic in our sense. We may first examine a *jury decision* as an example of weakest domination. We have already expressed this rule of social decision-making in the case of three individuals as

$$((\,((D_1,\, D_1,\, D^*)),\, ((D_2,\, D_2,\, D^*)),\, ((D_3,\, D_3,\, D^*)),$$
$$((-D_1,\, -D_2,\, -D_3))\,))$$

where D^* signifies

$$((-D_1,\, -D_2,\, -D_3,\, ((D_1,\, D_2,\, D_3))\,))$$

Our problem here is whether we can express this function only by votings, without resort to negations and constants. We can easily verify that a jury decision is monotonic and self-dual. It can be verified, however, that a jury decision is *not* strongly monotonic. Let us consider a society of three individuals and suppose that only one of the three individuals favours the issue, so that the social decision is indifference. Then suppose that another individual becomes a supporter of the issue. But the social decision is still an indifference because the third individual is still in opposition. This contradicts strong monotonicity. In spite of this information, however, we cannot yet arrive at a conclusion, because strong monotonicity is only sufficient for faithful representation.

However, we may note the following property of democracy. If a social decision function is democratic, so that it can be expressed only by votings, then $D_i = D$ so far as $D_j = 0$ for all $j \neq i$. It can easily be verified that the rule of jury decision does not satisfy this property. Thus we can state:

Theorem 3–15: The rule of jury decision cannot be expressed only by votings, in other words, a jury decision is not a democracy in our sense.

A jury decision cannot be equivalent to any compound of one-half majority rule. The above theorem has clarified that a jury decision is alien to an ordinary one-half majority rule.

Another social decision-making rule to be tested is the *one-half quorum rule*, by which we mean that a social decision can be made only if less than one-half of the individuals abstain; otherwise, a social decision is an indifference. This rule is seen to be self-dual but not monotonic. For suppose that two-fifths of the individuals in a society favour a certain issue, another two-fifths abstain, and the other one-fifth are against the issue. Then the society favours the issue. But suppose that all individuals against the issue change their attitude and abstain. Then, by the one-half quorum rule, the society's decision becomes an indifference. This is inconsistent with monotonicity. Therefore:

Theorem 3–16: The one-half quorum rule is not a democracy in our sense.

As shown in the above counter-example, the one-half quorum rule does not faithfully reflect a change in individual decisions; a social decision may change in an opposite direction to a change in individual decisions as a whole. It may also be noted that the same is true with any quorum rule, say, a two-thirds quorum rule, which means that a social decision ensues only if less than one-third of the individuals abstain. The trouble is not with the size of the quorum but with the idea of a quorum itself.

The following examples are obviously undemocratic: a *traditional society* (inconsistent with self-duality), a dictatorship (contradicts our nondictatorial condition). They are undemocratic in our sense, as well as in any possible sense of the word.

To some people, democracy according to our definition may appear too restrictive. For we exclude such familiar rules as jury decision or quorum rule. However, it can be seen that our definition of democracy and the ensuing argument suggest that those familiar rules contain something alien to the principle of majority voting. On the other hand, some may argue that our definition of democracy is too wide, because every possible combination of voting procedures is allowed. In actual practice, however, voting procedures are often combined in various complicated ways. In the United States, people vote on issues as members of a party, say the Democratic party, against members of another party, say the Republican party, on many occasions—presidential elections, senatorial elections, congressional elections, gubernatorial elections and so on. Thus, a particular social decision can be expressed only as an intricate compound of voting procedures. We had better, therefore, make allowances for the various possible combinations of votings rather than restrict ourselves to textbook cases. Our formulation of democracy may be thought of as a reasonable attempt to depict this familiar and dominant form of social decision-making.

Suggested Reading

Bryce, J.: *Modern Democracies* (1921)

Dahl, R. A.: *A Preface to Democratic Theory* (1956)

Arrow, K. J.: *Social Choice and Individual Values*, 2nd edn. (1964)

May, K. O.: 'A set of independent necessary and sufficient conditions for simple majority decision', *Econometrica* (1952)

Hu, Sze-Tsen: *Threshold Logic* (1965)

Chapter Four

DEMOCRACY IN A WORLD OF MORE THAN TWO ALTERNATIVES

1. Extended Definition. In the last chapter we presented our definition of democracy where there are only two alternatives. In the present chapter we shall try to extend the definition to cases involving more than two alternatives. Democracy in this generalized setting may be formulated and analysed in various ways. In this book, we shall adopt the following 'indirect approach'.

In a world of two alternatives, *democracy* has been defined as that kind of social decision function which is at least self-dual, monotonic and nondictatorial. In this chapter we shall first extend these three *desiderata* of democracy to a setting of more than two alternatives, and then define a democracy in this generalized setting also as a social decision function satisfying at least those three extended properties.

In fact, we shall discover that the extension of each democratic prerequisite is not unique, depending on the way in which the increase in alternatives is introduced into the formulation; the extended concepts will range from the weaker version to the stronger one. In the following, we shall try to consider every possible combination of the various forms of our basic *desiderata*. In particular, the rest of this book will be mainly concerned with the necessary conditions for democracy and with its possible inconsistencies, so that we shall pay special attention to a set of the weakest versions of our basic conditions. The next three sections will extend each of our three prerequisites in turn.

2. Neutrality. First, we shall try to extend the concept of *self-duality* to cases of more than two alternatives. For convenience of exposition, we now introduce a notation with the help of which we link a world of two alternatives to that of more than two alternatives. Let us denote by $D_j(x, y)$ the jth individual's decision concerning a pair of alternatives (x, y) taken in this order. Similarly, $D(x, y)$ denotes the society's decision concerning the same ordered pair. $D_j(x, y)$ or $D(x, y)$ assumes the values 1, 0, -1 accordingly as the jth individual or the society makes the decision xP_jy, xI_jy, yP_jx or xPy, xIy, yPx respectively. Evidently, $D_j(x, y) = -D_j(y, x)$ and $D(x, y) = -D(y, x)$.

The first type of extension of self-duality may now be given. D_j and D'_j signify two possibly different decisions of the jth individual. D and D' stand for two social decisions corresponding to the two combinations of the individual decisions; $D_1, D_2, \ldots, D_n$ and $D'_1, D'_2, \ldots, D'_n$.

> *Definition* (self-duality): A social decision function is called *self-dual*, if the social decision on any pair of alternatives is reversed, when all individual decisions are reversed on that pair and remain unchanged concerning any other alternatives:

$$(x)(y)\{(j)[(D_j(x, y) = D'_j(y, x))$$
$$. \; (z)\{(x \neq z \neq y) \supset (D_j(x, z) = D'_j(y, z))\}$$
$$. \; (z)(w)\{(x \neq z \neq y) \; . \; (x \neq w \neq y) \supset (D_j(z, w)$$
$$= D'_j(z, w))\}]$$
$$\supset [D(x, y) = D'(y, x)]\}$$

The reader will easily see that this definition is a natural extension of self-duality in the setting of two alternatives.

However, we interpreted self-duality in a world of two alternatives as impartiality with respect to alternatives. The above condition only requires a social decision function to be 'neutral' within each pair of alternatives; the function is 'neutral' to a change from (x, y) to (y, x) but may not be 'neutral' to a change from (x, y) to, say, (y, z). If we formulate neutrality in terms of more than two alternatives, we have:

Definition (neutrality): A social decision function is called *neutral*, if it has the same structure concerning any pair of alternatives:

$$(x)(y)(u)(v)\{(j)[(D_j(x, y) = D'_j(u, v))$$
$$. \; (z)\{(x \neq z \neq y) \; . \; (u \neq z \neq v) \supset (D_j(x, z)$$
$$= D'_j(u, z)) \; . \; (D_j(z, y) = D'_j(z, v))\}$$
$$. \; (z)(w)\{(x \neq z \neq y) \; . \; (u \neq z \neq v) \; . \; (x \neq w \neq y)$$
$$. \; (u \neq w \neq v) \supset (D_j(z, w) = D'_j(z, w))\}]$$
$$\supset [D(x, y) = D'(u, v)]\}$$

In other words, the permutation of the alternatives on the individual ballots induces the same permutation in the social decision. A neutral social decision depends only upon how the alternatives are ranked, not upon how the alternatives are labelled.

Now we have two extensions of self-duality in the case of two alternatives. Obviously, we can state:

Theorem 4–1: Neutrality implies self-duality, but not *vice versa*.

If there are only two alternatives, neutrality is equivalent to self-duality, but otherwise two properties yield different social decision-making rules.

3. Monotonicity. Similarly, let us try to extend the concept of *monotonicity* to cases of more than two alternatives.

Definition (monotonicity): A social decision function is called *monotonic*, if

$$(x)(y)\{(j)[(z)(D_j(x, z) \leqq D'_j(x, z))$$
$$. (z)(w)\{(z \neq x \neq w) \supset (D_j(z, w) = D'_j(z, w))\}]$$
$$\supset [D(x, y) \leqq D'(x, y)]\}$$

In other words, if every individual's decision concerning an alternative x remains unchanged or changes in favour of x and his decision concerning any other alternatives is unchanged, then a social decision concerning x also remains unchanged or changes in favour of x. This property may be regarded as a natural extension of monotonicity in the case of two alternatives, though other extensions are possible. In fact, this extension is, in essence, equivalent to K. J. Arrow's Condition 2, which we shall introduce in the next chapter.

Similarly, strong monotonicity can be extended.

Definition (strong monotonicity): A social decision function is called *strongly monotonic*, if the following two conditions hold:

$$(x)(y)[\{(\exists j)[D_j(x, y) < D'_j(x, y)]$$
$$\cdot (j)[(z)\{D_j(x, z) \leqq D'_j(x, z)\}$$
$$\cdot (z)(w)\{(z \neq x \neq w) \supset (D_j(z, w) = D'_j(z, w))\}]\}$$
$$\supset \{(D(x, y) = 0 \text{ or } 1) \supset (D'(x, y) = 1)\}]$$

and

$$(x)(y)[\{(\exists j)[D_j(x, y) > D'_j(x, y)]$$
$$\cdot (j)[(z)\{D_j(x, z) \geqq D'_j(x, z)\}$$
$$\cdot (z)(w)\{(z \neq x \neq w) \supset (D_j(z, w) = D'_j(z, w))\}]\}$$
$$\supset \{(D(x, y) = 0 \text{ or } -1) \supset (D'(x, y) = -1)\}]$$

This condition is the same as its counterpart in the case of two alternatives, except for the proviso that every individual's decision concerning any other alternatives be unchanged.

4. Nondictatorship and Symmetry. The third prerequisite for democracy is nondictatorship. The extension of this concept may take various forms according to the size of the sets of alternatives by which dictatorship is defined. For example, if an individual can impose his preference on the society concerning only one pair of alternatives, he can be said to be a dictator in the weakest sense.

Definition (weakest dictator): An individual is called a *weakest dictator*, if there exists one pair of alternatives on which his preference is always adopted by the society:

$$(\exists x)(\exists y)\{(D_j(x, y) \neq 0) \supset (D_j(x, y) = D(x, y))\}$$

where an individual in question is called the jth individual.

The dictator, of this definition, dominates the society only partially, so that he may not deserve the name of 'dictator'. In most countries, ownership of private property can be transferred only if the present owner consents. An owner is a dictator on the issue concerning the disposal of his private property. He is a weakest dictator in our present definition.

The antipodal definition is obviously as follows:

Definition (strongest dictator): An individual is called a *strongest dictator*, if, for any pair of alternatives, his preference is always adopted by the society:

$$(x)(y)\{(D_j(x, y) \neq 0) \supset (D_j(x, y) = D(x, y))\}$$

where the individual in question is the jth individual.

This definition may be too strong to express accurately the authority of a dictator in any existing cases of authoritarian rule. However, we now have two extreme types of dictatorship, between which all possible degrees of dictatorship exist. The various types of dictatorship can be arranged in an order of logical strength, or in an order of the size of the subsets of alternatives on which dictatorship is defined.

The nondictatorial condition varies in accordance with variations in the definition of dictatorship. The strongest nondictatorial condition can be induced if a weakest dictator is prohibited.

Definition (strongest nondictatorship): A social decision function is called *nondictatorial in the strongest sense*, if there is no weakest dictator.

The other extreme is as follows:

Definition (weakest nondictatorship): A social decision function is called *nondictatorial in the weakest sense*, if there is no strongest dictator.

Some readers might find either of these two definitions too extreme to delineate a nondictatorial society. In that case, they may consider a nondictatorial society as one which falls between these two extremes.

Nondictatorship is a kind of *egalitarian* condition in the sense that an extreme form of inequality called dictatorship is not allowed. We can, furthermore, conceive various types of egalitarian condition. Among them, the strongest egalitarian condition is the following extension of symmetry in cases of two alternatives.

> *Definition* (symmetry): A social decision function is called *symmetric*, if $F(R_1, \ldots, R_i, \ldots, R_j, \ldots, R_n) = F(R_1, \ldots, R_j, \ldots, R_i, \ldots, R_n)$ for all i, j $(i, j = 1, 2, \ldots, n)$.

In other words, a social decision function treats all individuals in a neutral manner. It is evident that symmetry implies nondictatorship in any sense.

5. Generalized Definition of Democracy. In the last chapter we defined a democracy as a social decision-making rule composed of and only of voting procedures. In a world of two alternatives we had no serious difficulty in defining a voting as well as a democracy. In a world of more than two alternatives, however, there is a serious difficulty in defining a voting in an unambiguous way so as to determine a democracy, as we shall show in the following sections. Let us, therefore, start by defining a democracy through analogy with the case of two alternatives. We shall later re-examine this particular meaning of democracy.

First, through analogy with Theorem 3–11, a necessary condition for democracy faced with an arbitrary number of alternatives may be given as a conjunction of the weakest versions of our three basic conditions:

> A social decision function is a democracy, only if the function is self-dual, monotonic and nondictatorial in the weakest sense.

A democracy is required to treat the alternatives in an impartial way, to let a social decision respond positively to individual decisions, and to treat the individuals in a sufficiently egalitarian manner. As was already noted, each basic condition has stronger versions so that the requirement could be more imposing. For example, self-duality may be replaced by neutrality. Nondictatorship may be of stronger types. However, this book will be concerned mainly with the above weakest form of necessary condition. The condition presents the minimum requirement for a democracy.

Then, through analogy with Theorem 3–12, the following strongest versions of three *desiderata* may be regarded as a sufficient condition for a democracy:

> A social decision function is a democracy, if the function is neutral, strongly monotonic and symmetric.

The condition should be regarded as the maximum requirement.

Let us now define a democracy as a social decision function satisfying a certain logical condition which is stronger than the necessary condition given above, and weaker than the sufficient condition just introduced.

This generalized definition of democracy is tentative and clearly incomplete; we have only specified an area in which the necessary and sufficient condition for democracy is to be located. However, we shall be, in the rest of this book, mainly concerned with necessary conditions for democracy and with a possible inconsistency inherent in it so that this incompleteness will not affect our following analysis.

In the following sections, we shall examine several actual examples of social decision-making rules which are ordinarily regarded as 'democratic'. It will be shown that our formal definition of democracy by means of analogy is, in fact, satisfied by those actual examples. In the course of our argument concerning a specific example called *finite ranking rule*, our definition of democracy will be re-examined.

6. Rules of Election. In a world of two alternatives, the most typical example of democracy is probably *simple majority voting* or *direct democracy*. Let us try to discover its counterpart in cases of more than two alternatives. However, the extension of simple majority voting has various versions, just as the extension of three basic conditions for democracy. We may classify those various extended rules of direct democracy into two types; the *overall comparison type* and the *piecemeal comparison type*.

We must exactly formulate these two concepts which will play the crucial role in the following analysis. Overall comparison roughly means that a social decision concerning all alternatives is made once and for all; a social decision cannot—at least in some cases—be broken down into the decisions concerning the subsets of alternatives.

Definition (overall comparison): A social decision is said to be based on *overall comparison*, if there is some proper subset of alternatives such that a social decision concerning the proper subset depends on individual decisions concerning all alternatives.

A proper subset of alternatives is any subset other than the set of all alternatives. Any other type of social decision function than the overall comparison type will be said to be *based on piecemeal comparison*. By piecemeal comparison we roughly mean that a social decision concerning a proper subset of a certain size depends only on the individual decisions concerning that proper subset, as if there were no other alternatives. An important special case of piecemeal comparison is *pairwise comparison*, in which a social decision concerning every pair of alternatives depends on and only on the individual decisions concerning that pair, and a social decision, as a whole, is given as a juxtaposition of those pairwise decisions.

In this section, as well as in the subsequent two sections, we shall introduce several examples of the overall-comparison-type extension of simple majority voting, most of which are, in fact, recognizable as various rules of election. For convenience of exposition in this chapter, let us consider a particular society composed of three individuals, faced with an issue consisting of three alternatives, a Labour candidate, a Liberal candidate and a Conservative candidate. Let us further suppose that three individual voters make the following decisions:

The first individual prefers La to Li and Li to Con.
The second individual prefers La to Li and Li to Con.
The third individual prefers Con to Li and Li to La.

La, Li and Con are short for Labour, Liberal and Conservative, of course. This particular combination of individual decisions is chosen to illustrate different social decisions according to different rules of election.

The most familiar example of the rules of election is probably *single-ballot voting*.

> *Definition* (single-ballot voting): A social decision function is called the rule of *single-ballot voting*, if the society ranks the alternatives according to the number of first preferences indicated by the voters.

In the example introduced above, the Labour candidate obtains the first preference twice, the Conservative obtains it once and the Liberal fails to reach it. Thus, according to this rule, the Labour candidate is ranked first by the society, the Conservative second and the Liberal third. A problem with single-ballot voting is that a candidate who is likely to occupy intermediate positions in individual decisions—such as the Liberal in the above example—suffers an unfavourable bias. In any country where single-ballot voting is adopted, a political party of eclectic nature is heavily handicapped, so that a two-party system will emerge.

However, such a bias is not inconsistent with the essentials of democracy. For we can easily verify:

> *Theorem* 4–2: The rule of single-ballot voting satisfies neutrality, monotonicity and symmetry, but not strong monotonicity.

It may be noted that the failure of strong monotonicity is due to the total neglect of any positions ranking lower than first preference.

Our attention is led naturally to the rule of *dual-ballot voting*.

> *Definition* (dual-ballot voting): A social decision function is called the rule of *dual-ballot voting*, if the society ranks the alternatives according to the number of first and second preferences which each voter indicates.

In the above example, the Liberal obtains three votes, the Labour candidate obtains two votes, and the Conservative obtains only one vote. The society now orders the Liberal as first, the Labour candidate as second, and the Conservative as third. The social decision is markedly different from the result obtained by single-ballot voting. Under dual-ballot voting, the second preference is given more importance; it is treated as exactly equal to the first preference. But in spite of this favouritism, the necessary condition for democracy is satisfied. We can easily verify

> *Theorem* 4–3: The rule of dual-ballot voting satisfies neutrality, monotonicity and symmetry, but not strong monotonicity.

The failure of strong monotonicity is due to the complete neglect of any preferences lower than the first or second, and to equal treatment of the first and second preferences.

We can similarly verify that any plural-ballot voting satisfies neutrality, monotonicity and symmetry, but not strong monotonicity. From our present formal point of view, single-ballot voting, dual-ballot voting and any plural-ballot voting equally satisfy the same version of the necessary condition for democracy, and equally fail to satisfy strong monotonicity.

63

However, an apparent inadequacy common to all these rules of election is their complete neglect of any lower-ranking preferences. For example, in the single- or dual-ballot voting, only the first or second preference is taken into consideration, while any of the lower-ranking preferences cannot influence the social decision. All those rules of election are based on 'limited information', so to speak. In the next section, we shall introduce a social decision-making rule based on 'full information'.

7. Finite Ranking Rule. The various rules of elections introduced above, indeed, satisfy our necessary condition for democracy. But they all take into account only some of the individual decisions, so that strong monotonicity is not guaranteed. In this section, let us consider a broader class of social decision-making rules, where generally all the details of individual decisions are taken into account in making a social decision.

In our familiar example, let us assign 3 points to the first preference, 2 points to the second preference, and 1 point to the third preference. Under this weighting rule, the Labour candidate collects 7 points from three individuals, the Liberal obtains 6 points, and the Conservative obtains 5 points. The society will then rank the three candidates according to their total points. The Labour candidate is now ranked first, the Liberal second and the Conservative last. This rule yields a different social decision from those under single- or dual-ballot voting.

This idea can be generalized. Let us suppose that there is an issue composed of a finite number of alternatives. Then, for each individual, let us assign a natural number to each alternative, so that the order of assigned numbers may preserve—or, at least, not reverse—the order of preference in his decision. The society shall rank all the alternatives according to the sum total of numbers assigned by all individuals. Every assigned number may be interpreted as a rank in each individual's preference ordering. We may call this class of social decision functions *finite ranking rule*. For a fuller discussion of finite ranking rule, the reader may refer to L. A. Goodman and H. Markowitz's work.

The finite ranking rule covers a great many examples. It must be noted that simple majority voting in a world of two alternatives is the simplest example, where any numbers may be assigned to the first and second preferences, as long as the first is assigned a greater number than that assigned to the second.

The various rules of election in the last section constitute a special class of finite ranking rule. Under those rules, an order of assigned numbers does not reverse, nor always preserve, an order of preference with respect to alternatives. We may call this particular class an *incomplete finite ranking rule*. If an order of assigned numbers strictly preserves an order of preference, a finite ranking rule may be called *complete*.

In a world of three alternatives, a complete finite ranking rule can be most typically constructed, as we did above, by assigning 3, 2 and 1 to the first, second and third preferences. But, evidently, this is not the only way; we might as well assign 5, 2 and 1 to the first, second and third preferences, so that particular importance is attached to the first preference. An actual example of a finite ranking rule is the usual method of team-scoring in a contest which is essentially individual, such as each nation's team-scoring in Olympic games.

In this fashion, a finite ranking rule can be applied to any number of alternatives, in so far as the number remains finite. In any case, except the case of two alternatives, however, a finite ranking rule has infinitely many versions, according to the ways of assigning numbers to the alternatives. Equivocality characterizes a finite ranking rule. Nevertheless, any one of these examples equally satisfies the basic desiderata for democracy. In particular, we have:

> *Theorem* 4–4: A complete finite ranking rule satisfies neutrality, strong monotonicity, and, if the same rule of assigning the numbers is applied to all individuals, symmetry.

A complete finite ranking rule satisfies the strongest version of our basic conditions for democracy.

In terms of the conditions for democracy, therefore, a complete finite ranking rule corresponds to simple majority voting in a world of two alternatives; both satisfy neutrality, strong monotonicity and symmetry. Thus, we may regard a complete finite ranking rule as the legitimate overall-comparison-type extension of simple majority voting. However, there is a marked difference. A finite ranking rule in a world of more than two alternatives has many versions, because there is no intrinsic criterion for choosing one among many possible ways of assigning numbers to alternatives; the resulting social decision can be, in some cases, almost arbitrary. On the other hand, simple majority voting has one unique form. In fact, it is a special case of a finite ranking rule, where any difference in the ways of assigning numbers cannot affect the resulting social decision.

In a realm of two alternatives, we abstracted from simple majority voting, and conceived a voting operator. In the present generalized setting, we might similarly conceive something like 'finite ranking operator'. Then we can define, analogously, a democracy as a social decision function consisting of and only of 'finite ranking operator'. This idea is possibly a starting point of an interesting field of study. But we shall not develop it in this book. However, one thing may be noted here. The above definition of democracy by means of a 'finite ranking operator' leads to the same conclusion as we derived before that self-duality, monotonicity and nondictatorship are necessary for democracy in the generalized sense. Our present indirect and analogical approach seems after all appropriate.

8. Representative System. In the last two sections, we have been trying to extend the concept of direct democracy to the setting of more than two alternatives. In this section, we shall investigate several examples of indirect democracy or representative system in a world of more than two alternatives. Let us consider, for example, a society in which each electorate adopts the rule of single-ballot voting. As explained before, this rule yields each electorate's preference ordering of the candidates. However, the election is not yet completed, because it has still to be determined how many representatives are actually to be returned. The same is true with the rule of dual-ballot voting or with any plural-ballot voting. They only determined the decision of the lowest committee called an electorate.

If one candidate is to be returned to a higher committee called, for example, the House of Parliament, that is, if only the first preference by each electorate is to be returned, such rule is usually called *small electorate system*. Small electorate system is formally equivalent to the rule of single-ballot voting in a higher committee, where each electorate is assigned only one vote.

In *large electorate system* where the seats to be filled are plural, not only the first preference, but also the second or several lower-ranking preferences will be elected. Large electorate system can be seen to be formally equivalent to some plural-ballot voting in a higher committee.

A representative system in a world of more than two alternatives may be roughly defined as a combination of a voting rule and an electorate system. The simplest example is probably single-ballot voting in a small electorate system. It may be regarded as a combination of single-ballot votings at two levels. So-called *complete plural-ballot voting* means the plural-ballot voting where the number of ballots is equal to the number of the seats to be filled in each electorate. In so-called *restricted plural-ballot voting*, the number of ballots given to each individual voter is smaller than the number of the seats to be filled. In these two examples, the rules of plural-ballot voting are combined at two levels.

All these rules of indirect democracy yield different patterns of social decision, so that the choice of the rules is the subject of heated debate among political scientists as well as politicians. However, we can verify, as before, that any of these rules satisfies neutrality, monotonicity and nondictatorship in the strongest sense, although not strong monotonicity nor symmetry. From our formal point of view, none of the rules can be thought of as more democratic than any other.

We must note that all the above rules are composed of *incomplete* finite ranking rules, such as single- or plural-ballot voting. In other words, they take into account only a part of each individual's decision as well as of each electorate's. Thus, political scientists devised the rule of *proportional representation* as a way of obtaining more information about individual decisions or of 'reducing dead votes'. Some of them even suggest that proportional representation is theoretically more 'democratic' than other types of representative system. But their assertion is not well founded.

There is not room in the space of this book to explain the intricate rules and practices of proportional representation; the interested reader should refer, for example, to Duncan Black's book. However, we can argue quite generally as follows. Is proportional representation superior to single-ballot voting in small electorate system? For that matter, is a particular rule superior to another rule when the latter collects less information about individual decisions than the former? If a social decision-making rule is to be evaluated according to an 'amount of information' it gathers, a complete finite ranking rule is unquestionably the best rule. However, as we have noted before, a finite ranking rule is marred by arbitrariness.

We may assign, for example, an overwhelming

weight to the first preference and almost infinitesimal weights to the other lower-ranking preferences. This particular complete finite ranking rule yields virtually the same social decision as single-ballot voting. If we agree that a complete finite ranking rule is the best conceivable, how can we assert that proportional representation is definitely better than single-ballot voting which is so close to a certain complete finite ranking rule?

The point is that, whether we collect information fully or not, we have no absolute principle for utilizing the information concerning individual decisions. For we have no intrinsic principle for expressing numerically the ranks in each individual's preference ordering. Neutrality demands that we treat all alternatives in an impartial manner. Symmetry demands that we treat all individuals in an equal manner. However, no principle within the democratic framework seems capable of telling us how to treat the ranks in individual orderings—of telling us what rule is better in this respect (for example, whether the rule of proportional representation is better than the rule of single-ballot voting).

9. Pairwise Comparison. In the last several sections, we have been investigating the overall-comparison-type extension of simple majority voting. We now proceed to the pairwise-comparison-type extension; the other piecemeal-comparison-type extension will be examined in the final chapter. Let us recall the example which we gave in Section 6 and have repeatedly utilized since. Under the pairwise-comparison-type extension of simple majority voting, the issue is broken down into three pairwise issues, that is, the

Labour candidate against the Liberal, the Liberal against the Conservative, and the Conservative against the Labour candidate. First, let three individuals vote on an issue, the Labourite against the Liberal. The first and second individuals vote for the Labour candidate, and the third individual votes for the Liberal. A social decision by simple majority voting on this issue is that the Labour candidate is preferred to the Liberal candidate. Similarly, the society prefers the Liberal to the Conservative on another issue, the Liberal against the Conservative. Lastly, the Labour candidate is socially preferred to the Conservative. Fortunately, the result in this case satisfies all axioms of preference ordering.

However, it is not always the case. We can conceive a case where:

The first individual prefers La to Li and Li to Con.
The second individual prefers Con to La and La to Li.
The third individual prefers Li to Con and Con to La.

The reader can easily verify that under the pairwise-comparison-type extension of simple majority voting the society prefers the Labour candidate to the Liberal, the Liberal to the Conservative and the Conservative to the Labour candidate. The social decision is circular so that it does not satisfy our Axiom 2, the transitivity of preference relation. A social decision under this rule is inconsistent in spite of the consistency of all individual decisions. This phenomenon is sometimes called a *voting paradox*. This is not an unexpected consequence. For a social decision under this rule is no more than the juxtaposed pairwise decisions, so that there is no guarantee that those pairwise comparisons are always consistent.

In the above example, the alternatives are three and the individuals are three. In fact, the minimum numbers yielding a voting paradox are, as the example in Section 6 of the final chapter shows, three alternatives and two individuals. If there are more than two alternatives, and more than one individual, and if each alternative is pitted against each of the other alternatives under the rule of simple majority voting, then an inconsistent social decision occurs for some combination of individual decisions. It must be noted, however, that a voting paradox may not be revealed if the number of the rounds of voting is limited. According to Duncan Black:

> *Theorem* 4–5 (Black's theorem): The existence of a voting paradox is always revealed if there are as many rounds of voting as there are alternatives.

Therefore, if there are three alternatives, three rounds of voting are sufficient to reveal a voting paradox, as is shown in the above example. If there are five alternatives, five rounds of voting are enough, although these five do not cover all the possible pairwise combinations among five alternatives. More generally, if a number of alternatives is equal to m, a number of all possible pairwise combinations of alternatives is equal to $m(m-1)/2$. Black's theorem assures us that we have only to vote at most m times to produce, if at all, an intransitive social decision.

An actual example of the pairwise-comparison-type extension of simple majority voting may be worth considering. In the U.S. House of Representatives (as well as the U.S. Senate), at most four amendments

72

to a bill are permitted, so that Congressmen may be faced with five alternatives at one time. Five alternatives are, for example, an original proposal, an amendment, an amendment to the amendment, a substitute amendment (which means an amendment to the first amendment), and an amendment to the substitute. After all the amendments are offered, the House votes first on the amendment to the amendment (versus the amendment), then on the amendment to the substitute (versus the substitute), then on the substitute (versus the amendment) and finally on the amendment (versus the original). According to the regulation, the House votes at most four times. The reader can easily verify that an intransitivity never appears under this procedural rule. But this does not mean that no intransitivity exists; it may just not be revealed. W. H. Riker, taking a particular case in the House of Representatives in 1953, ingeniously argued that an intransitivity is likely to be concealed. So far as it goes, this procedural rule is cunning, because it never reveals an intransitivity and so never results in a standstill of the legislative machine. However, it is another matter whether or not such a rule can reflect faithfully the individual decisions as a whole. We shall examine this problem in the next section.

Let us consider the example of the British House of Commons. This body votes as many times as the alternatives offered, so that an intransitive social decision can be revealed. However, the British two-party system is firmly established, so that an intransitive social decision can hardly occur, while an intransitivity is likely to exist in the American counterpart because of her inter-party and intra-party factions.

The pairwise-comparison-type extension of simple

majority voting has at least one merit. It produces a unique social decision concerning each pair of alternatives; there is no equivocality as we found in the overall-comparison-type extension. However, the pairwise-comparison-type extension has one serious demerit. A resulting social decision is intransitive for some combination of individual decisions. If an intransitivity is revealed, the society is confronted with a stalemate. Even if an intransitivity is concealed, the society may face an *instability* of social decision, which is the subject of the next section.

10. Stability of Social Decision. Throughout this book we generally assume that an individual's decision is equivalent to his preference, that is, that no individual makes a decision against his preference. In this section, we relax this assumption to allow every individual to make a decision against his preference or, in other words, to behave strategically or *insincerely*. Then we can introduce a concept of *stability of social decision* or, more exactly, *stability of the outcome of a social decision*. By stability of social decision we mean that neither an individual nor a group of individuals could achieve, by making a different decision, an outcome which he or all of them preferred. Without stability, a social decision is not likely to be reached, because some of the individuals are going to avoid, by adopting a more profitable strategy, an outcome of the social decision in question. In the general setting where strategic moves are permitted, a social decision cannot be meaningful without stability.

Let us start by formulating our stability concept in exact terms. We now need to distinguish an individual *decision* from an individual *preference*. Let us denote

74

the *j*th individual's preference by the same symbol as before: R_j, P_j or I_j, and his decision by the bold symbol: $\mathbf{R}_j$, $\mathbf{P}_j$ or $\mathbf{I}_j$. In this section we are assuming that $R_j \equiv \mathbf{R}_j$ does not necessarily hold, whereas we assume elsewhere in this book that $R_j \equiv \mathbf{R}_j$.

Several definitions are necessary for the following argument.

Definition (outcome): An alternative to which no other alternatives are preferred in a social decision $F(\mathbf{R}_1, \mathbf{R}_2, \ldots, \mathbf{R}_n)$ is called an outcome of the individual decisions $\mathbf{R}_1, \mathbf{R}_2, \ldots, \mathbf{R}_n$.

In other words, an outcome is an alternative to be chosen by the society. Now we can formulate a concept of stability which we have already introduced verbally.

Definition (stability): An outcome x of the individual decisions $\mathbf{R}_1, \mathbf{R}_2, \ldots, \mathbf{R}_n$ is called stable, if

$$\sim (\exists \mathbf{R}'_1)(\exists \mathbf{R}'_2) \ldots (\exists \mathbf{R}'_n)[(\exists_j)(\mathbf{R}_j \neq \mathbf{R}'_j) \\ . (j)\{(x'P_j x) \vee (\mathbf{R}_j = \mathbf{R}'_j)\}]$$

where x' is an outcome of the individual decisions $\mathbf{R}'_1, \mathbf{R}'_2, \ldots, \mathbf{R}'_n$.

This definition is a slight modification of M. Dummet and R. Farquharson's formulation and, in a wider perspective, a variation of stability concepts developed in the theory of games. The interested reader should refer to R. D. Luce and H. Raiffa's noted book *Games And Decisions*.

Let us first consider a simple majority voting based on pairwise comparison, and ask if such a social decision-making rule is stable. The following seemingly unstable example may be useful for understanding the present problem. Let us suppose that three individuals have the following individual preferences concerning an issue composed of three alternatives called La, Li and Con.

The first individual prefers La to Li and Li to Con.
The second individual prefers Li to Con and Con to La.
The third individual prefers Con to Li and Li to La.

Simple majority voting on the pair (La, Li) results in a social preference of Li to La. Similarly, Li is socially preferred to Con. Li is the most preferred alternative so that it is an outcome of *sincere* individual decisions.

Then let us suppose that the third individual does not vote according to his preference, and tries to manipulate the result in his favour. For this purpose, on the pair (La, Li) he votes for La against his preference. On the pair (La, Con) he votes for Con according to his preference. Simple majority votings on the pair (La, Li) and the pair (La, Con) result in the following social decision: Con is socially preferred to La and La is socially preferred to Li. Now Con seems to be the most preferred alternative or the new outcome, which, moreover, the third individual prefers to Li, the original outcome. The original outcome as a consequence of sincere votings seems to be unstable.

However, this is not the case. For, once the society votes on another pair (Li, Con), the society prefers Li to Con; any strategic move on the side of the third individual cannot alter this result. It can now be seen that the social decision as a whole is intransitive, so that there exists no most preferred alternative, that is, no outcome. Therefore, the third individual's strategic move cannot produce the new *outcome* which is to replace the original outcome. Then, by definition, the original outcome of the sincere individual decisions is stable.

This example teaches us two lessons. In the first place, the minority's—in the above example, the third individual's—decision can be adopted as a 'social decision', if simple majority voting is not undertaken on all possible pairs of alternatives or, in other words, if the so-called round robin process is not completed. As an actual example, the procedural regulation in the U.S. House of Representatives restricts a number of the rounds of voting so that the minority opinion may possibly be adopted through the ingenious manoeuvre on the side of minority. The completion of the round robin process may be considered as essential to pairwise simple majority voting, if we want to avoid the minority rule under a possibility of insincere votings.

The second lesson is that pairwise simple majority voting may be subject to the strategic manipulation of a group of individuals to the extent that a transitive social decision can be transformed into an intransitive one. The minority can be influential enough to evade the definite outcome and replace it by a stalemate.

As a matter of fact, the rule of pairwise simple majority voting can secure a stability for any *sincere* individual decisions—so far as those individual decisions always result in a transitive social decision. This may be held to be one of the significant virtues of simple majority voting. However, such virtue will be lost if the round robin process of voting is not completed. It is true that a restriction on a number of the rounds of voting can conceal an irrationality of social decision so that a stalemate can be avoided. But such restriction will, in some cases, render a social decision unstable. Transitivity and stability constitute a dilemma.

In fact, a similar property can be established with regard to a more general class of social decision functions based on pairwise comparison. For we can prove:

> *Theorem* 4-6: Suppose that a social decision function is based on pairwise comparison. An outcome of the sincere individual decisions is always stable, if and only if the underlying social decision function is monotonic.

(necessity): Suppose that a social decision function is not monotonic. Hence, for some pair of alternatives (x, y) there exist two combinations of the sincere individual decisions $D = F(D_1, D_2, \ldots, D_n)$ and $D' = F(D'_1, D'_2, \ldots, D'_n)$, called the first situation and the second situation, such that $D > D'$ when $D_j = D'_j$ for a group of individuals, called group A, and $D_j < D'_j$ for a group of remaining individuals, called group non-A. D, D' or D_j, D'_j signify the social or individual decisions on the pair (x, y) taken in this order.

Let us then construct the third situation in the following way. Group non-A can be divided into two groups; a group of the individuals for whom xI_jy holds in the first situation is called group B, and a group of the individuals for whom yP_jx holds in the first situation is called group C. Then consider a combination of such individual decisions that the individual decisions in groups A and B remain the same as in the first situation and those in group C are the same as in the second situation. This situation is called the third situation and is signified by D'' $= F(D''_1, D''_2, \ldots, D''_n)$. $D''_j = D_j$ for groups A and B, and $D''_j = D'_j$ for group C. D'' may take any value. The case can be distinguished; case (1) $D'' > D'$ and case (2) $D > D' \geqq D''$.

Case (1). Let us compare the second and third situations. They differ only in group B, for which xP_jy holds in the second situation, and xI_jy holds in the third situation. Then an outcome y in the second situation cannot be stable. For group B could have obtained, by adopting the insincere individual decisions equal to xI_jy, an outcome x which they preferred to y. Case (2). Let us compare the first and third situations. They differ only in group C, for which yP_jx holds in the first situation and xI_jy or xP_jy holds in the third situation. Then an outcome x in the first situation cannot be stable. For group C could have obtained an outcome y by behaving as if they were in the third situation. *Q.E.D.*

The proof of sufficiency is easy so that it is left to the reader. Dummet and Farquharson tackled a problem similar to our Theorem 4–6, although their orientation is a little different. It is now to be recalled that a democracy has been defined as a social decision function which is at least monotonic. Therefore, if a democracy is based on pairwise comparison, the outcome of sincere individual decisions is, if it exists at all, always stable. Any insincere or strategic move cannot improve the situation for any individual. This is one of the essential features of democracy based on pairwise comparison. Therefore, in so far as a democracy is based on pairwise comparison, a distinction between individual decisions and individual preferences may not be so important. Our general assumption of an equivalence between decision and preference is to this extent justified.

We should now proceed to examine the stability of a social decision function based on overall comparison. However, no general statement can be established in the case of overall comparison; our statements have to be specific. For example, the reader can easily verify that, under single-ballot voting, the outcome of sincere individual decisions is always stable. On the other hand, it is not the case with any plural-ballot voting, nor with a finite ranking rule. Stability seems to be a rare virtue among democratic rules based on overall comparison so that single-ballot voting is to be highly esteemed in this respect. Finally, let us suggest the following statement but leave it, in this book, as a conjecture: Monotonicity is necessary for the stability of an outcome of sincere individual decisions under *any* social decision functions.

Our stability analysis in this section is, in fact, an application of a similar analysis developed in the field of the theory of games. However, our stability concept, as well as similar concepts in the theory of games, are far from satisfactory. For one thing, we only consider a manipulation by one group. Many groups of individuals may well try to manipulate a social decision in their favour by various strategies, and the interaction of many different moves will yield a very complicated result. An analysis of such cases is beyond the scope of this book and, for that matter, of the theory of games at the present stage of development.

Throughout this chapter we have been concerned with a democracy in a world of an arbitrary number of alternatives. Compared with our approach in the last

chapter, our approach in this chapter is tentative
rather than conclusive; many points have still to be
further examined. The present attempt will, the author
hopes, be the first step to a more rigorous analysis.
Finally we may note that our classification of democracy into two types—overall comparison and pairwise comparison—is more than a mere analytical
convenience. In the following two chapters, we shall
tackle the problem of voting paradox in its widest
sense, where the classification in question will play a
crucial role.

Suggested Reading

Dahl, R.: *A Preface to Democratic Theory* (1956)

Black, D.: *The Theory of Committees and Elections*
(1958)

Goodman, L. and Markowitz, H.: 'Social Welfare
Function Based on Individual Rankings', *American Journal of Sociology* (1952)

Riker, W. H.: 'The Paradox of Voting and Congressional Rules for Voting on Amendments',
American Political Science Review (1958)

Dummett, M. and Farquharson, R.: 'Stability in
Voting', *Econometrica* (1961)

Luce, R. D. and Raiffa, H.: *Games and Decisions*
(1957)

Chapter Five

VOTING PARADOX

1. Arrow's Generalization. If a simple majority voting is taken on each pair of alternatives, a social decision as the juxtaposition of those pairwise comparisons is not always transitive. As we mentioned before, this phenomenon is called *voting paradox*. Knowledge of voting paradox is centuries old; we can trace it back to Condorcet, an eighteenth-century French encyclopaedist. Quite recently, K. J. Arrow made a remarkable contribution to the subject, proving that the same phenomenon can be observed in a more general class of social decision function, though like many economists Arrow preferred the term *social welfare function* to our term social decision function. This chapter is devoted to an introduction of his work.

On the social welfare function, or on the social decision function, Arrow imposes five conditions which aim at rendering the function 'democratic'. We shall now present these five conditions in our own terms which are, in fact, not far from Arrow's original formulation.

Condition 1 (collective rationality): An issue includes some triple of alternatives, on which every possible combination of individual decisions actually occurs within the domain of the social decision function. It should be recalled that every decision —individual as well as social—is an ordering satisfying Axioms 1, 2 and 3.

Up to this point, we have been implicitly assuming that every possible combination of individual decisions over the whole issue actually occurs within the domain of social decision functions, in so far as the axioms of ordering are satisfied. From now on, we shall take into account the possibility of a restricted domain. Under Arrow's Condition 1, a restricted domain is allowed; a freedom of individual decisions is guaranteed only in a particular triple of alternatives. Condition 1 is weaker than the condition of complete freedom, which we have been implicitly assuming and we shall later call Condition 1'.

Arrow calls his Condition 2 the condition of positive association of social and individual values.

Condition 2 (positive association):
$$(x)(y)\{(j)[(z)(D_j(x, z) \leq D'_j(x, z))$$
$$. (z)(w)\{(z \neq x \neq w) \supset (D_j(z, w) = D'_j(z, w))\}]$$
$$\supset \{(D(x, y) = 1) \supset (D'(x, y) = 1)\}\}$$

Evidently, Arrow's Condition 2 is a special case of our monotonicity; the former is logically weaker than the latter.

The third condition is crucial to voting paradox.

Condition 3 (independence of irrelevant alternatives): Take any subset of an issue. If $D_j(x, y) = D'_j(x, y)$ for all j and for all pairs of alternatives in that subset, then the socially most-preferred alternative (or alternatives) in that subset remains unchanged.

This condition is equivalent to the following:

Condition 3 (binary choice or pairwise comparison):
For any pair of alternatives, a social decision
depends on, and only on, the individual decisions
concerning that pair.

Individual decisions concerning any other pairs are
irrelevant to this determination. Arrow requires that a
social decision be based on pairwise comparison.

The fourth condition is called citizen's sovereignty.

Condition 4 (citizen's sovereignty): For any pair of
alternatives (x, y), there exists a combination of
individual decisions which induces xPy and there
exists a combination of individual decisions which
induces yPx.

In other words, a social decision can never be fixed for
any pair of alternatives. The reader can easily verify
that our 'self-duality' implies Arrow's Condition 4,
unless a social decision is always an indifference for
some pair of alternatives.

Finally, Arrow imposes:

Condition 5 (nondictatorship): There is no individual
whose preference is always adopted by the society,
for any pair of alternatives.

This condition is obviously equivalent to our nondictatorship condition in the weakest sense.

Let us now recall our argument and, particularly,
our definition of democracy in a world of two alternatives, because Arrow assumes a principle of pairwise
comparison. Then, we can assert

Theorem 5–1: A democracy based on pairwise
comparison satisfies Arrow's five conditions.

We should note that, for any pair of alternatives, a social decision cannot be always indifference, as far as a democracy based on pairwise comparison is concerned. We have shown that Arrow's conditions are, indeed, necessary conditions for democracy.

2. General Possibility Theorem. Arrow tried to establish that these five conditions are not consistent, or that a social decision function satisfying these five conditions is not 'generally possible'. In the first edition of his book, *Social Choice and Individual Values*, he presented a 'general possibility theorem' which shows, in his own words, 'that, if no prior assumptions are made about the nature of individual orderings, there is no method of voting which will remove the paradox of voting':

> *Arrow's theorem:* If there are at least three alternatives, there is no social decision function satisfying Conditions 1, 2, 3, 4 and 5.

However, J. H. Blau later pointed out that Arrow's theorem is correct only if there are exactly three alternatives; in the following sections, we shall prove this modified version of Arrow's theorem. But, if we now tentatively assume that Arrow's theorem holds for exactly three alternatives, we can easily reinstate his original contention. For, instead of Condition 5, we may as well impose a slightly stronger nondictatorial condition.

> *Condition 5'*: Among the triples of alternatives satisfying Condition 1, there is at least one triple on which no individual is a dictator.

Now Conditions 1 and 5' together guarantee the

existence of a triple of alternatives, under which no individual is a dictator. Then, by virtue of Condition 3, we can regard this triple as a whole issue and disregard any other alternatives. Thus, an inconsistency can be proved for this triple, so *a fortiori* we have:

Theorem 5–2: If there are at least three alternatives, there is no social decision function satisfying Conditions 1, 2, 3, 4 and 5'.

In fact, this theorem is one extreme expression of a more general statement. The other extreme, proved by Blau, is an easy corollary of Theorem 5–2:

Theorem 5–3: If there are at least three alternatives, there is no social decision function satisfying Conditions 1', 2, 3, 4 and 5,

where Condition 1 is replaced by the condition of complete freedom, that is:

Condition 1': All possible combinations of individual decisions concerning all alternatives actually occur in the domain of the social decision function.

In this version of Blau, Condition 1 is strengthened up to Condition 1', while Condition 5 remains untouched. On the other hand, in Theorem 5–2, Condition 5 is reinforced up to Condition 5', whereas Condition 1 is left untouched.

Indeed, the above two statements lead to the following more general statement:

Theorem 5–4: Suppose that there are at least three alternatives. If there exists a subset composed of more than two alternatives on which no individual is a dictator and on which all possible combinations

86

of individual decisions actually occur, then there is no social decision function satisfying Conditions 2, 3 and 4.

The reader may note that these three theorems— Theorems 5–2, 5–3 and 5–4—are, in fact, equivalent; each one implies another one. The statement takes various forms according to the size of the subset of alternatives on which 'freedom' of individual decision and nondictatorship coexist. If the size of the subset in question is reduced to a triple of alternatives, we have Theorem 5–2. If the size coincides with a whole issue, the set of all alternatives, then Theorem 5–3 can be inferred. The reader may note that the freedom of individual decision condition and the nondictatorship condition are inversely related so to speak.

It may now be argued that Arrow's main contention has been reinstated in the form of Theorem 5–4, in spite of the failure of his first attempt. A social decision function which is 'democratic' in Arrow's sense cannot exist. Therefore, a *democratic* social decision function based on pairwise comparison in our sense cannot exist, because Arrow's set of conditions—say, condition 1', 2, 3, 4 and 5—is definitely weaker than any version of our necessary condition for democracy. A voting paradox occurs not only in simple majority voting, but also in any democratic decision, so far as it is based on pairwise comparison. *Generalized voting paradox* can now be established, if Arrow's theorem does hold in the case of exactly three alternatives or— which is equivalent—if any one of the above three theorems holds. In the following sections, we shall investigate several logical properties of Arrow's 'democratic' social decision function, and finally prove

Arrow's original contention in the form of Theorem 5–3.

3. Monotonicity and Unanimity Rule. In deriving several important properties of Arrow's social decision function, we intend to prove that Arrow's five conditions defining the function are inconsistent. From inconsistent premises, we can derive any statement whatsoever. Any property of Arrow's social decision function is meaningful only if it is derived from those of the five conditions which are mutually consistent. It is imperative to specify from what conditions a property in question is deduced.

Let us first examine Arrow's Condition 2 and the related concepts. As we mentioned before, Condition 2 is slightly weaker than our monotonicity, in the sense that the former concerns only a social preference while the latter makes a statement not only for social preferences but also for social indifferences. The difference is due to the fact that Arrow was interested in proving the inconsistency, rather than in presenting a complete formulation.

Theorem 5–5: Monotonicity implies Arrow's Condition 2.

If Condition 2 is coupled with Condition 3, the condition of pairwise comparison, we may consider a simpler formulation introduced by Blau:

Condition 2′ (Blau):

$$(x)(y)[(j)\{D_j(x, y) \leq D'_j(x, y)\} \supset \\ \{(D(x, y) = 1) \supset (D'(x, y) = 1)\}]$$

Then, obviously follows:

Theorem 5–6: Under Condition 3, Condition 2′

implies Condition 2. However, the converse is not always true, because a domain of the function may possibly be so limited that

$$(\exists x)(\exists y)(\exists j)[\{D_j(x, y) \le D'_j(x, y)\} \supset (\exists z)\{(z \ne x) \\ \supset (D_j(z, y) \ne D'_j(z, y))\}]$$

We can assert that:

Theorem 5–7: If Conditions 1′ and 3 hold, then Condition 2′ is equivalent to Condition 2.

Let us next consider a property called *unanimity rule of preference*:

Definition (unanimity rule of preference): If all individuals prefer an alternative x to an alternative y, then the society prefers x to y:

$$(x)(y)\{(j)(xP_jy) \supset xPy\}$$

In terms of *decisive group*, we can define the same concept as follows:

Definition (unanimity rule of preference): A group of all individuals is decisive for any pair of alternatives.

It will be generally agreed that the unanimity rule of preference is an essential characteristic of a democracy.

Concerning Arrow's social decision functions, we can assert:

Theorem 5–8: Condition 2 and Condition 4 together imply the unanimity rule of preference.

Proof: Condition 4 guarantees that there be some combination of individual decisions which induces xPy concerning the pair (x, y). Then suppose that all individual decisions change, if necessary, to xP_jy concerning the pair (x, y), by raising the position of x in the individual orderings. By Condition 2, a social decision remains xPy. *Q.E.D.*

Similarly, we can establish:

Theorem 5–9: Monotonicity and self-duality together imply the unanimity rule of preference, unless the social decision is always an indifference.

We have now established that the unanimity rule of preference is one of the necessary conditions for democracy.

We may here note that unanimity rule of preference implies Condition 4, if Condition 1′ holds, but it does not imply Condition 2 even under Condition 1′. For we can conceive the following social decision function for every pair of alternatives:

$$((D_1, D_2, -D_3))$$

which follows the unanimity rule of preference, but does not satisfy Condition 2. Conditions 2 and 4 provide a stronger set of conditions than the unanimity rule of preference.

4. Neutrality. We now proceed to examine a neutrality of Arrow's social decision functions. Arrow, as well as Blau, proved:

Theorem 5–10: If Condition 1′, Condition 3 and the unanimity rule of preference hold, then a social decision function is identical for any pair of alternatives, so far as no individual indifferences occur.

Or, if Condition 1′, Condition 3 and the unanimity rule of preference hold, then:

$$(x)(y)(u)(v)[(j)\{(D_j(x, y) \neq 0) . (D'_j(u, v)$$
$$\neq 0) . (D_j(x, y) = D'_j(u, v))\}$$
$$\supset \{D(x, y) = D'(u, v)\}]$$

Proof: For some pair of alternatives (x, y), take an arbitrary combination of individual decisions. Suppose that the resulting social decision is xRy; the case where yRx occurs can be dealt exactly in the same way. Then classify all individuals into two groups V' and V'' such that xP_jy for all j in V', and yP_jx for all j in V''. Consider the following combination of individual decisions concerning three distinct alternatives (x, y, w):

xP_jy and yP_jw for all individuals in V'
yP_jw and wP_jx for all individuals in V''

By the unanimity rule of preference, yPw. Then by the transitivity of social decision, xPw holds for a combination of individual decisions such that xP_jw for all j in V', and wP_jx for all j in V''.

Then, similarly, consider three distinct alternatives (x, v, w) and the following individual decisions:

vP_jx and xP_jw for all individuals in V'
wP_jv and vP_jx for all individuals in V''

By the unanimity rule of preference, we have vPx. Then by the transitivity of social preference, vPw holds for such combination of individual decisions that vP_jw for all j in V', and wP_jv for all j in V''.

Similarly, for three distinct alternatives (u, v, w), we can prove that uPv holds for such combination of individual decisions that uP_jv for all j in V', and vP_ju for all j in V''.

Then, if we apply the same argument to a change from the pair (u, v) to the pair (x, y), we have xPy for

G   91

such combination of individual decisions that xP_jy for all j in V', and yP_jx for all j in V''. Therefore, xRy cannot be xIy, but xPy. Thus, we have proved the theorem. *Q.E.D.*

In other words, Arrow's social decision function is neutral to a change of alternatives, in so far as individual indifferences do not occur. It may be noted that a social indifference does not occur as long as individual indifferences do not occur. We may call this type of neutrality a *quasi-neutrality*.

Arrow's social decision function is only quasi-neutral, but not neutral. In order to secure neutrality, we need two slightly stronger properties than the unanimity rule of preference.

Definition (strong unanimity rule of preference):

$$(x)(y)[\{(j)(xR_jy) . (\exists_j)(xP_jy)\} \supset xPy]$$

Definition (unanimity rule of indifference):

$$(x)(y)\{(j)(xI_jy) \supset xIy\}$$

In other words, if all individuals who do not abstain prefer x to y, then the society prefers x to y. If all individuals are indifferent between x and y, then the society is also indifferent between x and y. These two properties are fairly strong. Not only does Arrow's social decision function lack these properties but also a monotonic and self-dual social decision function sometimes fails to follow the strong unanimity rule of preference. But, a democracy in a world of two alternatives satisfies these properties, as is obvious from the nature of its construction.

However, if these two properties are satisfied, neutrality can be derived.

Theorem 5–11: If Condition 1′, Condition 3, the strong unanimity rule of preference, and the unanimity rule of indifference hold, then the social decision function is neutral.

The proof is similar to the proof of Theorem 5–10 so it is left to the reader. The following theorem, in particular, is a by-product of the proof:

Theorem 5–12: If Condition 1′, Condition 3, the strong unanimity rule of preference, and the unanimity rule of indifference hold, then a social indifference occurs only when all individuals are indifferent.

We now see that Arrow's social decision function or democratic social decision function based on pairwise comparison must have the same or almost the same structure concerning any pair of alternatives. This result is, as the reader may have noted, due to the transitivity of social preference, and becomes quite understandable in view of the conclusion reached in the next section.

5. Emergence of Dictator. We have already introduced the concept of *decisive group* in Chapter Two. Here, we introduce a slightly weaker but similar concept.

Definition (quasi-decisive group): A group of individuals V is called *quasi-decisive* for a pair of alternatives (x, y) if

$$[\{(j\in V) \supset xP_jy\} \,.\, \{(j\notin V) \supset yP_jx\}] \supset xPy$$

Evidently, a decisive group is always quasi-decisive. But the converse is not always true. We can assert:

Theorem 5–13: If Condition 2 and Condition 3 hold,

a quasi-decisive group for a pair of alternatives is decisive for that pair.

The proof is obvious. However, Condition 2 is not necessary for the equivalence between decisiveness and quasi-decisiveness. For we can prove:

Theorem 5–14: Suppose that there are at least three alternatives. If Condition 1', Condition 3 and the unanimity rule of preference hold, then a quasi-decisive group for a pair of alternatives is decisive for any pair of alternatives.

Proof: Suppose that a group of individuals V is quasi-decisive for a pair of alternatives (x, y). Consider the following combination of individual decisions concerning three distinct alternatives (x, y, z):

xP_jy and yP_jz for all individuals in V or,
yP_jx and yP_jz for all individuals not in V

By the unanimity rule of preference, we have yPz. Then by the transitivity of social decision, xPz holds regardless of the decisions of the individuals not in V concerning a pair of alternatives (x, z). Therefore, V is decisive for the pair (x, z). Then by similar reasoning, V is decisive for any pair. *Q.E.D.*

We are now in a position to prove that a decisive group is, in Arrow's setting, reducible to a single individual or, in other words, the existence of a decisive group implies the existence of a dictator.

Theorem 5–15: Suppose that there are at least three alternatives and that Condition 1', Condition 3 and the unanimity rule of preference hold. If a decisive group exists for some pair of alternatives, then a dictator in the strongest sense exists.

Voting Paradox

Proof: Suppose that V is a minimal decisive group for a pair of alternatives (x, y); since a decisive group exists, such a minimal group must exist. Let j be a particular individual in V, W the remaining individuals in V, and U the group of individuals not in V. Let z be any third alternative distinct from x or y, and consider the following combination of individual decisions.

xP_jy and yP_jz for the jth individual,
zP_kx and xP_ky for all individuals in W,
yP_kz and zP_kx for all individuals in U

Then xPy holds, because V is supposed to be decisive for the pair (x, y). Suppose that zPy holds. This would mean that W is quasi-decisive for the pair (z, y). By Theorem 5–14, W is decisive for the pair (x, y). This contradicts the minimality of V. Then suppose that zPy does not hold. This means yRz. By transitivity of social decision, xPz holds. Then the jth individual is quasi-decisive for the pair (x, z). By Theorem 5–14, he is decisive for any pair of alternatives. These consequences can be consistent, only if the minimal decisive group includes only one individual. *Q.E.D.*

In the light of this theorem, our neutrality theorem —Theorem 5–10—can now be clearly understood. Arrow's social decision function is quasi-neutral in the sense that a particular individual's preference always becomes a social preference. Arrow's social decision function is, in fact, dictatorial, and therefore quasi-neutral. Two properties—quasi-neutrality and dictatorship—should always be coupled in Arrow's social decision functions.

We now know that a dictator must emerge in order

95

to achieve an invariably transitive social preference. The requirement of transitive social decision is so imposing that only a dictator can overcome the difficulty of possible intransitivity.

6. Generalized Voting Paradox. We now proceed to present a theorem stating a generalized voting paradox. The unanimity rule of preference implies that a group of all individuals is decisive for any pair of alternatives. This implies, by Theorem 5–15, the existence of a dictator in the strongest sense. The existence of such a dictator contradicts Arrow's Condition 5, the nondictatorship condition. Therefore, we have Blau's version:

Theorem 5–3: If there are at least three alternatives, there is no social decision function satisfying Conditions 1′, 2, 3, 4 and 5.

However, if we carefully trace a sequence of proofs, Conditions 2 and 4 are effective only through the unanimity rule of preference. Therefore:

Theorem 5–16: If there are at least three alternatives, there is no social decision function satisfying Conditions 1′, 3, the unanimity rule of preference, and Condition 5.

The prototype of this theorem is due to K. Inada, in which he replaces Condition 5 by his own version of nondictatorial condition.

Inada's nondictatorship condition: There is no individual whose preference is adopted by the society, for any pair of alternatives, in spite of all other individuals' opposition.

96

Voting Paradox

In our terms, it requires that no individual be quasi-decisive for any pair of alternatives. However, by virtue of our Theorem 5–14, this nondictatorship condition is equivalent to Condition 5. Inada's theorem is, in fact, equivalent to Theorem 5–16. Condition 1' and Condition 5 in Theorem 5–16 may be replaced by Condition 1 and Condition 5', respectively. More generally, Theorem 5–16 can be generalized, as Theorem 5–3 is generalized in Theorem 5–4. All in all, Theorem 5–16 inclusive of these variations is the strongest statement that has so far been made concerning the generalized voting paradox, although we shall present an even stronger statement in the next chapter. However, Theorem 5–16 adequately shows that a 'democratic' social decision function in Arrow's sense cannot exist. The general possibility of Arrow's generalized voting is completely excluded.

Moreover, we can assert in line with the analysis of this book:

Theorem 5–17: A democracy based on pairwise comparison cannot exist in a world of more than two alternatives.

This theorem is an easy corollary of Theorem 5–16. The general possibility of democratic social decision function based on pairwise comparison is now denied. If a democracy is based on pairwise comparison, there is no other way than dictatorship to secure the transitivity of social decision in the face of all possible combination of individual decisions. Only at the cost of transitivity of social decision, can a democracy satisfy all of its fundamental prerequisites. Thus a democracy is confronted by a dilemma, in so far as it adopts the principle of pairwise comparison.

Suggested Reading

Arrow, K. J.: *Social Choice and Individual Values*, 2nd edn. (1964)

Blau, J. H.: 'The Existence of Social Welfare Functions', *Econometrica* (1957)

Guilbaud, G. T.: 'Les Théories de L'intérêt Général et la Problème Logique de L'agrégation', *Economie Appliquee* (1952)

Inada, K.: 'Alternative Incompatible Conditions for a Social Welfare Function', *Econometrica* (1955)

Chapter Six

VOTING PARADOX
RECONSIDERED

1. The Meaning of the Voting Paradox. The argument
in the last chapter tells us that a 'voting paradox' can
be found not only in *pairwise simple majority voting*,
but also in any *democratic* social decision functions
based on *pairwise comparison*. We may now further
inquire whether or not the same phenomenon occurs
in a still wider class of social decision functions than a
democracy based on pairwise comparison. Indeed,
even Arrow's original proof established an inconsistency for that set of conditions which is weaker than a
democracy by our definition. We are led to doubt that
Arrow's set of conditions is the weakest that can in-
duce an inconsistency.

In fact, we already know that Arrow's set of conditions is not the weakest set, in that sense. Theorem
5–16 established that a similar but different set of
conditions, which may be called Inada's set of conditions, involves an inconsistency. Inada's set of conditions consists of Arrow's Condition 1, Condition 3,
Condition 5 and the unanimity rule of preference. As
the unanimity rule of preference is definitely weaker
than Conditions 2 and 4, Inada's condition is weaker

than Arrow's condition. We must now ask what kind of society Inada's set of conditions symbolizes.

For this purpose, let us consider the following example. Suppose that a society consists of three individuals and adopts the rule of pairwise simple majority voting. Then let us suppose that the society uses a voting machine which, however, is out of order so that the decision of the third individual is registered as its opposite. Consequently, a social decision is given as

$$((D_1, D_2, -D_3))$$

The resulting social decision can hardly be thought of as democratic in any sense of the term. For, in spite of the support of the majority composed of the second and third individuals, the social decision takes the side of opposition; symbolically, $D_1 = -1$, $D_2 = 1$ and $D_3 = 1$ implies $D = -1$. The reader can easily verify that this social decision-making rule satisfies the unanimity rule of preference, but not Arrow's Condition 2, which is almost equivalent to monotonicity. Generally speaking, under Inada's conditions, a social decision function may be based on the minority principle. Theorem 5–16 asserts that a 'voting paradox' occurs under this type of social decision function which is not sufficiently democratic. It may now be suggested that a 'voting paradox' inheres not only in simple majority voting, not merely in a democracy even, but also in a far broader class of social decision functions.

2. Extension of the Voting Paradox. Although Inada's set of conditions falls considerably short of democracy, it still retains some democratic flavour in the form of the unanimity rule of preference. In this section, we consider whether the unanimity rule of preference is essential to a 'voting paradox'. With the unanimity rule of preference replaced by Condition 4, we can assert, to begin with:

Theorem 6–1: Suppose that there are at least three alternatives. If Conditions 1′, 3 and 4 hold, then either the unanimity rule of preference or the anti-unanimity rule of preference holds for any pair of alternatives; i.e.: one and only one of the following holds for any pair of alternatives:

(1) $(j)(xP_jy) \supset xPy$,
(2) $(j)(xP_jy) \supset yPx$

Proof: Suppose that, for some pair of alternatives (x, y), xP_jy for all j. Three types of social decision are conceivable, that is, xPy, xIy and yPx. Let us now examine the first case, which is that of the unanimity rule of preference concerning the pair (x, y). Then let us take the third alternative z, distinct from x and y, and consider the pair (z, x). By virtue of Conditions 3 and 4, there exists a combination of individual decisions concerning the pair (z, x) which yields zPx. Further, let us consider a combination of individual decisions concerning the pair (z, y) such that zP_jy for all j. It can be seen that the individual decisions concerning three pairs (x, y), (z, x) and (z, y) are all consistent. The social decision concerning the pair (z, y) is zPy by the transitivity of social decision. Then the unanimity rule of preference holds for the pair (z, y). By similarly rotating a pair of alternatives, we can establish that the unanimity rule of preference holds for any pair of alternatives, if the rule holds for some pair.

Then consider the second case, that of the anti-unanimity rule of preference, or, xP_jy for all j implies yPx. Then take a pair (z, x) for which we can find, by Conditions 3 and 4, a combination of individual decisions which yields xPz. Then, by the same reasoning as before, for a pair (z, y), zP_jy for all j implies yPz, which is the anti-unanimity rule of preference. In this second case, it can be established that the anti-unanimity rule of preference holds for any pair, if such a rule holds for some pair.

Finally, let us consider the third case where xP_jy for all j implies xIy. But this is impossible. For, by arguing as in the first case, it follows that zP_jy for all j implies zPy. This in its turn implies that xP_jy for all j implies xPy. This is a contradiction. *Q.E.D.*

According to this theorem, Condition 4 implies, under the transitive social decision, either the unanimity rule of preference or the anti-unanimity rule of preference. It must be noted that we obtain this result without the help of Condition 2, or of monotonicity in our sense. In view of this result, we substitute for Condition 5 the following condition:

Condition 5″ (nondictatorship and nonpersecution): There is no individual whose preference is always adopted by the society for any pair of alternatives, and there is no individual whose preference is always opposed by the society for any pair of alternatives:

$$(j)\ \{(\exists x)(\exists y) \sim [\{D_j(x, y) \neq 0\} \supset$$
$$\{D_j(x, y) = D(x, y)\}]$$
$$.\ (\exists u)(\exists v) \sim [\{D_j(u, v) \neq 0\} \supset$$
$$\{D_j(u, v) = -D(u, v)\}]\}$$

This condition requires that no individual be so powerful as to be a dictator, and no individual be so persecuted that the society adopts a principle of opposing always his decision.

Then the proof of the following extended theorem is straightforward:

Theorem 6–2: If the alternatives are at least three, there is no social decision function satisfying Conditions 1', 3, 4 and 5''.

Proof: First note that there are only two cases, that in which the unanimity rule of preference holds for any pair of alternatives, and that in which the anti-unanimity rule of preference holds for any pair. In the first case, our theorem is equivalent to Theorem 5–16. In the second case, where the anti-unanimity rule of preference holds, let us fictitiously define an artificial social decision xQy as equivalent to yPx. The anti-unanimity rule of preference becomes the unanimity rule of preference under the newly defined social decision. The condition of nonpersecution in Condition 5'' similarly becomes the condition of nondictatorship. Then Theorem 5–16 ensures that the social decision symbolized by xQy is not always transitive. Evidently an intransitivity of xQy is equivalent to an intransitivity of xPy. *Q.E.D.*

Condition 5'' is stronger than Condition 5. Therefore, it seems that Theorem 6–2 is not stronger than Theorem 5–16. However, as the proof of Theorem 6–2 shows, the theorem is a juxtaposition of two statements; the first statement is Theorem 5–16, and the second statement is a, so to speak, inverse version of Theorem 5–16 whose essence is roughly a contradiction between the anti-unanimity rule of preference

103

and the condition of nonpersecution. As the two statements are independent, we may assert that Theorem 6–2 is virtually an extension of Theorem 5–16.

Theorem 6–2 concerns a very broad class of social decision functions. In analogy with mathematics, Condition 4 means that the function does not take on a constant value, while Condition 5″ prohibits the case where the function is always equal to a particular independent variable or to it with the opposite sign. In other words, a social decision function cannot be reduced to a constant or to a particular independent variable, and so must be *nontrivial* as a function. Theorem 6–2 may even be read as follows:

> If the alternatives are at least three, there is no *nontrivial* social decision function based on pairwise comparison.

We may thus conclude that the paradox is not simply of a voting, nor even of a democracy based on pairwise comparison, but of any nontrivial social decision-making rule based on pairwise comparison. The paradox is inherent in any problem of aggregating many ordering relations into a single ordering, but not in any particular form of aggregation, such as a democracy. The voting paradox may now be rechristened the paradox of ordering aggregation or, simply, the paradox of social decision.

It may now be presumed that Theorem 6–2 is possibly the strongest statement as far as Condition 4 and Condition 5 (or 5″) are concerned. The relaxation of either of these two conditions will cause our general possibility theorem to fail. No one would doubt that a dictatorial society makes a consistent decision if and only if the dictator is consistent, and a traditional

104

society makes a consistent decision if and only if the traditional decision is consistent. We shall now proceed to attempt a relaxation of the other two conditions, Condition 1′ and Condition 3.

3. Farewell to Pairwise Comparison. Although, the relaxation of Condition 4 or of Condition 5 (or 5″) dissolves the paradox, at the same time it renders the whole problem trivial. On the other hand, the relaxation of the remaining two conditions—Condition 1′ and Condition 3—can lead us to a meaningful dissolution of the paradox. This section, as well as the next, will deal with Condition 3, while Sections 5 and 6 will be concerned with Condition 1′.

Condition 3 which we called the condition of *pairwise comparison* concerns 'quality and quantity of information' required to arrive at a social decision. For the fuller understanding of Condition 3, we may break down the condition into the following two requirements:

Condition 3-a (condition of pairwise determination): For any pair of alternatives, a social decision depends on and only on the state of information concerning that pair,

and

Condition 3-b (condition of ordinal preference): For any subset of alternatives, the state of information consists of and only of all individuals' decisions represented as preference orderings concerning that subset.

Condition 3-a states that, if a society tries to make a

decision for any pair of alternatives, it has to collect information concerning only that pair. Any information regarding other pairs is irrelevant. Condition 3-a may be interpreted as a restriction on the range or 'quantity' of the information needed to make a social decision.

Condition 3-b demands, on the other hand, that the society consider only individual preference orderings, and discard any other kind of information about individual decision. For example, some individual may barely prefer an alternative x to an alternative y, whereas another individual may strongly prefer y to x. A society might be tempted to consider these preference intensities. However, Condition 3-b requires the society to ignore those differences in preference intensity. This condition may be interpreted as a restriction on the content or 'quality' of information to be referred to in social decision-making.

These two separable conditions are lumped together into Condition 3. As we shall show in the next section, the two requirements are indeed logically related. But they are—at least primarily—concerned with different aspects of social decision-making. The distinction between the two sides of Condition 3 is important for understanding a basic difference between the two approaches which we are going to present as a means for dissolving the paradox—the overall comparison approach and the cardinal utility approach. In this section, we shall investigate the former approach, relaxing Condition 3-a.

We have established in Section 2 of this chapter that there exists no nontrivial social decision function based on *pairwise comparison*. It must be recalled that pairwise comparison is only a special case of piecemeal comparison. For example, we may consider *trinary comparison* by which we mean that a social decision concerning a triple of alternatives depends on and only on the individual preference orderings concerning that triple; any social decision can be broken down into trinary comparisons, but no longer into pairwise comparisons. The introduction of trinary comparison is an immediate relaxation of Condition 3-a. But the following argument will show that trinary comparison is not a remedy.

Let us consider, for example, an issue composed of four alternatives (x, y, z, w), and suppose that some social decision function based on trinary comparison is given. First, let us take a triple (x, y, z). Then, for every combination of individual decisions concerning this triple, the given rule provides a social decision which may be expressed as $D^1(x, y)$, $D^1(y, z)$ and $D^1(x, z)$. Similarly, the rule determines a social decision concerning another triple (y, z, w) which may be shown as $D^2(y, z)$, $D^2(z, w)$ and $D^2(y, w)$. However, $D^1(y, z)$ and $D^2(y, z)$—the results of two distinct, trinary comparisons—can be always consistent, only if such trinary comparison is reduced to a pairwise comparison. For, if $D^1(y, z)$ and $D^2(y, z)$ are identical, then a social decision concerning the pair (y, z) becomes independent of the individual decisions concerning the pairs (x, y) and (x, z) on the one hand, and the pairs (z, w) and (y, w) on the other. A social decision concerning the pair (y, z) depends solely on the individual decisions concerning that pair, in other words, is based on pairwise comparison. The reader may note that the same argument can be applied to any pair of alternatives. Therefore, a social decision function based on trinary comparison, if it is to be always consistent, has to be reduced to a social decision function based on pairwise comparison.

We can generalize this argument. In a world of more than four alternatives, a consistent quaternary comparison is reduced to a trinary comparison, which is, in its turn, reduced to a pairwise comparison. With the aid of Theorem 6–2, similar reasoning leads to:

Theorem 6–3: Suppose that there are at least three alternatives and they are well-ordered. A social decision function based on piecemeal comparison cannot satisfy all of Conditions 1′, 4 and 5″.

If alternatives are infinitely many but not well-ordered, we have to modify the definition of piecemeal comparison so as to reinstate Theorem 6–3. But here we shall not be involved in such technical subtlety. Theorem 6–3 is the ultimate version of 'general possibility theorem'. Guilbaud and Inada have suggested similar conclusions, though in different settings.

We could therefore say that, in order to dissolve the paradox of social decision, we are bound to abandon any piecemeal comparison whatsoever for overall comparison. Overall comparison is necessary for dissolving the paradox, in so far as the other conditions —including Condition 3-b—remain unrelaxed. A question to be answered now is whether overall comparison is sufficient or, in other words, whether we can always construct a social decision function based on overall comparison, thereby avoiding the paradox. To fully answer this question, we have to distinguish two types of problems: In the first place, is such overall comparison *logically possible*? Secondly, is such overall comparison not only logically possible, but *actually workable*?

The answer to the first question is in the affirmative. We can construct an artificial social decision-making rule which dissolves the paradox according to the basic idea of *finite ranking rule*, if certain regularity conditions are satisfied. For convenience of exposition, we shall present the rule in connection with Hildreth's proposal, to be considered in the next section. However, it should be emphasized that a construction of such social decision function is possible, only if a society is *fully* informed of individual decisions or, in other words, only if all individuals' preference ordering concerning *all* alternatives are known to a society. Any partial information is insufficient. An overall comparison which dissolves the paradox is logically possible, if a society is thus fully informed.

We then turn to the second question of actual workability. By actual workability we do not mean institutional efficiency or organizational flexibility, which is obviously imperfect in any actual society. The present formal analysis is not at all concerned with such empirical problems. However, we may conceive the following workability notion which is formal in character and so relevant to our present analysis.

Overall comparison presupposes a society's knowledge of individual decisions concerning all alternatives. Then we may raise a question as to how the society can obtain such knowledge. It may be assumed that the society can obtain it only through each individual's overt action such as voting; we should not expect any society to have some 'introspective' means for collecting such information. Thus, workability of a social decision-making rule may be defined to mean that necessary information can be expressed and conveyed in the form of a *finite* number of individual overt actions or, in other words, in the form of a *finite* number of signals issued by each individual. If the information necessary for a social decision includes an *infinite* number of signals, we may term such a rule *unworkable*, for reception of such an infinite sequence of signals could never be completed in a finite length of time.

In our argument, an *issue* may be any type of set; it may include a finite number of alternatives, or infinite number of them. If an issue is of finite size, our workability problem can be seen to raise no difficulty; an individual preference ordering concerning a finite number of alternatives can be expressed at most by a finite number of individual overt actions. For example, a particular class of issues called *elections* involve only a relatively small number of alternatives called *candidates*. In any actual rules of election, a society collects sufficient information through voters' ballots, bringing all candidates into a once-for-all comparison. It can easily be seen that any rules of election presented in Chapter Four are based on overall comparison and satisfy Condition 1', 2, 4 and 5''. In an issue composed of a finite number of alternatives, an overall comparison is not only possible, but also workable so that the paradox in question can be dissolved.

However, if an issue includes infinitely many alternatives, we are likely to be confronted by difficulty. For necessary information in this case may be expressed only by infinitely many signals. True, there are some exceptionally amenable cases. For example, if each individual can always designate his first preference, second, third and so on, among infinitely many alternatives, then some rule of *plural ballot voting* is applicable. Necessary information in this case includes only a finite number of signals. However, this is not always the case. In ordinary economic theories of consumer behaviour, for example, the consumer can select no such first preference, second preference, third and so on among possible expenditure plans; the interested reader should refer to any textbook of economics. In any attempt to aggregate such individual consumers' decisions—which may be duly called 'welfare economics'—the information needed would be infinite. For another example, we may consider, as many social scientists do, democracy in general rather than in a particular issue. Democracy in this generalized view has to be ready for any intractable cases where an infinite amount of information would also be required.

We may now conclude that collecting the information required to make an overall comparison is *not always workable*, for the required information may be obtainable only through infinitely many signals from each individual. Therefore, a dissolution of the paradox by means of overall comparison is indeed logically possible, but may not be workable in some important issues composed of infinitely many alternatives. Some readers may find a resemblance between our present argument and K. R. Popper's well-known assertion that we cannot verify any universal statement about infinitely many possible events.

If we try to guarantee the workability of a social decision function, we have to avoid an overall comparison. Arrow's Condition 3 may be regarded as an attempt to secure workability for any issues. The paradox of social decision is, therefore, due to a society's actual inability to make an overall comparison in any cases. If a society were supposed to be omniscient in this sense, the paradox would disappear. However, such dissolution is not practicable at all.

4. Intensity of Preference. We have generally assumed in this book that an individual's decision is nothing more nor less than his preference ordering on alternatives. Few would deny that ordinality of preference is an essential element of consistent individual decisions. Particularly, it has been an accepted fact in modern economic analysis that ordinal preference theory is sufficient, as well as necessary, for rationalizing economic choice behaviours in static situations. As such theory is sufficient, any additional assumptions are to be regarded as superfluous. In other disciplines such as political science, however, individual decisions are often considered as something more than preference orderings. In this section, we shall try to introduce an additional attribute of individual decisions, and so modify Condition 3-b and the related arguments.

As we suggested in the last section, an individual might be capable not only of ordering the alternatives according to his preference, but also of comparing *preference intensities* with respect to alternatives. For example, Mr. Jones might feel that he passionately prefers a Conservative candidate to a Liberal candidate, whereas he barely prefers the Liberal to a Labour candidate. Like Mr. Jones, we sometimes feel that we can differentiate among preference intensities. Moreover, we may conceive a society where the minority prefers an alternative much more ardently than the majority prefers the contrary alternative. We may well doubt that the majority principle still makes sense. It is worth while trying to include preference intensity as an admissible element of individual decisions, and also as a factor in social decision-making.

The concept of preference intensity may be more rigorously formulated as follows. Let us take a quadruple of alternatives (x, y, z, w) in an issue. We have been assuming that an individual orders those alternatives according to his preference—say, he prefers x to y and z to w. For an introduction of preference intensity, we further assume that he is capable of telling whether the degree to which he prefers x to y is greater, equal or smaller than the degree to which he prefers z to w. In other words, the individual is assumed to *order*—in the sense of the *axioms of ordering* presented in Chapter One—not only the alternatives themselves but also the 'intervals' between any pair of alternatives.

If the preference intervals are thus completely ordered, it logically follows that we can construct a numerical index representing the preference intensity, as well as the preference order. In other words, the jth individual can be associated with a real-valued function $U_j(x)$, such that he prefers an alternative x to y if and only if $U_j(x) > U_j(y)$, and he prefers x to y more intensely than he does z to w, if and only if $U_j(x) - U_j(y) > U_j(z) - U_j(w)$. As a matter of fact, such function is not fully unique, but it is unique up to monotone linear transformation; the function may have different origins and different units of measurement, but otherwise it is uniquely determined. According to the tradition of economics, this kind of function may be called a *cardinal utility index*.

To be more exact, the above numerical representation needs assistance from a 'regularity' condition called the Archimedean property. The meaning of Archimedean property is, in fact, relevant to the workability of the numerical representation, and so of the following attempt to dissolve the paradox of social decision. In this book, however, we shall not explore this subtle question. The interested reader should refer, for example, to J. S. Chipman's article.

Along with the above 'preference interval' hypothesis, we may also introduce *expected utility hypothesis*, which can similarly derive a cardinal utility. The hypothesis may be roughly stated as follows. When faced with alternatives involving risk, the individual will choose that alternative for which the mathematical expectation of satisfaction is greatest. It then follows, as before, that the individual can be associated with a cardinal utility index which he behaves as though he were maximizing. This is, in fact, another way of introducing the concept of preference intensity. For fuller understanding of expected utility hypothesis, the reader should refer to Luce and Raiffa's book.

Under either of these two hypotheses, the individual's decision can be numerically represented. However, the origin and unit of measurement of preference intensity is, as we noted, arbitrary. As we choose the Fahrenheit system or the Centigrade system in measuring temperature, so we have to determine the origin and unit of measurement here. In other words, we have to select two 'base' alternatives, such as freezing point and boiling point in the Centigrade system, for which the magnitudes of utility are artificially fixed.

114

Now let $U_1, U_2, \ldots, U_n$ and $U'_1, U'_2, \ldots, U'_n$ be two sets of individual cardinal utility indices, representing different individual decisions, where $U_j(x)$ or $U'_j(x)$ is to be thought of as uniquely determined, by selecting two base alternatives. Then a state of information with respect to each alternative can be expressed by these individual cardinal utility indices. Thus, as Rothenberg suggested, Condition 3-b may be replaced by:

Condition 3'-b: For any subset of alternatives, the state of information consists of, and only of, all individuals' cardinal utility indices with respect to the alternatives in that subset.

Accordingly, Condition 3 may be replaced by:

Condition 3': Take any subset of an issue. If $U_j(x) = U'_j(x)$ for all individuals and for all alternatives in that subset, then the corresponding social decisions concerning that subset are identical.

Condition 3' is a natural consequence of our introduction of preference intensity as an admissible element of individual decisions.

It can easily be seen that Condition 3'-b relaxes Condition 3-b. Moreover, it must be noted that Condition 3-a, the condition of pairwise determination, is also relaxed in Condition 3'. For an individual cardinal utility function $U_j(x)$ has been determined by fixing artificially the magnitudes of utility at two base alternatives, so that two base alternatives are, in fact, always brought into comparison. A cardinal utility index $U_j(x)$ represents the information concerning *at least three* alternatives.

115

If every individual's decision is thus represented as a uniquely determined cardinal utility function, we can easily construct a social decision function which can aggregate individual decisions. The proposed rule of social decision-making is simply that all alternatives should be ordered according to the magnitudes of 'social utility index' defined as a summation of all individuals' cardinal utility indices.

As a matter of fact, C. Hildreth presented a fairly plausible example of such rule on the assumption that every individual behaves according to an expected utility hypothesis, and he proved that his example satisfies Condition 1', 2, 3', 4 and 5. His rule includes, among other things, a trick for determining base alternatives for each individual utility index. This implies that an arbitrary principle of numerical inter-personal comparison is being adopted. As in the case of *finite ranking rule*, such arbitrariness is inevitable in this latter-day version of Bentham–Edgeworth's utility calculus.

In passing, we wish to complete our argument of the last section. If a society is informed of every detail of all individuals' preference orderings, then the society can artificially construct, for each individual, a cardinal utility function consistent with his preference ordering. Then we can conceive, in Hildreth's fashion, a social decision function which avoids the paradox, even if there exist no *intrinsic* individual cardinal utility indices. It is important to note that, if the society is informed of only a part, but not the whole of the alternatives, we cannot construct an individual cardinal utility index which can guarantee, over the whole issue, a consistency with his preference ordering.

Let us return now to the argument of this section. Hildreth's example established that formally the paradox of social decision can be dissolved if every individual's decision includes not only preference orders but also preference intensities. However, we have to question, as before, the workability of such a social decision-making rule or, in other words, how a society could be informed of every individual's cardinal utility index. We may now pose two questions. In the first place, we may wonder whether every individual has the introspective ability to measure his own preference intensity in numerical terms. Secondly, we may wonder—even if every individual were capable of so measuring introspectively—how a society could obtain access to the numerical values of these individual cardinal utility indices.

The first question itself is controversial. Would Mr. Jones be able to evaluate a Conservative candidate, a Liberal candidate and a Labour candidate in numerical terms, say, as 100, 50 and 10 respectively—although the origin and unit of measurement is in itself arbitrary? Would his numerical representation always be consistent? Many people would be sceptical of such introspective ability. But this is mainly an empirical question.

However, even assuming tentatively such introspective ability, we would find difficulty in designing a suitable procedure, such as voting, to collect the necessary numerical information. Few can expect Mr. Jones to reveal his utility evaluation as it is on his 'ballot sheet'. He can be expected to overstate a preference intensity concerning the alternative he prefers, for instance, the Conservative candidate. Such *insincere* action is likely to be profitable in any procedure

117

analogous to voting. In terms of Section 10 of Chapter Four, a voting involving numerical expressions is likely to be unstable. Numerical voting is logically possible, even workable in our sense, but may be held to be impractical because of its instability.

We might be able to by-pass this impasse, if a society could objectively measure each individual's cardinal utility index. Such indirect measurement is indeed possible in experimental situations, as Freedman–Savage, Mosteller–Nogee and Davidson–Suppes demonstrated. But it is highly doubtful that such an experiment could be successfully carried out in actual practice. Particularly, if an issue includes infinitely many alternatives, the feasibility of such an experiment is formally equivalent to the workability of overall comparison, about which we were so critical in the last section. Objective measurement of felt preference intensity is not always workable.

We should admit that felt preference intensity is sometimes a fact. In many political situations, we feel an urge to incorporate differences in preference intensity into a social decision. R. A. Dahl's political analysis will be suggestive in this respect. However, the trouble is that we may not be able to measure, directly or indirectly, intensities of sensations. Moreover, we cannot hope to establish any social decision-making rule to cope with problems of preference intensity. In summarizing our argument in this section, as well as in the last, we may conclude that a dissolution of the paradox of social decision via relaxation of Condition 3 is, though logically possible, impractical, at least in many circumstances. In retrospect, Condition 3 may be regarded as a condition to ensure that a social decision function is always practicable.

118

5. Similarity among Individual Decisions. We have
generally assumed in this book that individual decisions can take any form, in so far as they satisfy
the axiom of ordering. In terms of Arrow's analysis,
this assumption is called Condition 1'. In this section,
we shall introduce the possibility of restricted individual decisions, or a relaxation of Condition 1'.
Under Condition 1', the individual decisions can be
of any form, for example, the form xP_1y and yP_1z for
the first individual, and yI_2z and yP_2x for the second
individual. For convenience of exposition, we may
graphically represent their individual decisions as in
Fig. 1.

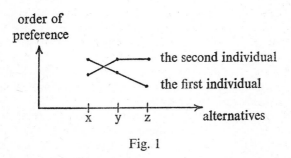

order of
preference

the second individual

the first individual

x   y   z   alternatives

Fig. 1

The relative height represents a preference-ordering
of three alternatives in each individual decision. An
arrangement of the alternatives on the horizontal axis
is arbitrarily made. A pairwise simple majority voting
by these two individuals produces an intransitive
social decision such that xIy, yPz and xIz.

Similarly, we may consider a society of three
individuals whose decisions are respectively xP_1y

119

and yP_1z, yP_2z and zP_2x, and zP_3x and xP_3y. The graphical representation is as follows:

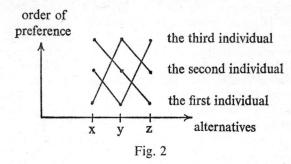

Fig. 2

The social decision as a consequence of pairwise simple majority voting is intransitive—xPy, yPz and zPx. As the above two examples suggest, a voting paradox occurs only if some strong dissimilarity exists among the individual decisions or, stated in visual terms, in their profiles. The dissimilar individual decisions cause the paradox.

Many might argue that one of the essential features of a democracy is that the process of persuasion or of assimilation takes place before an actual decision, say, voting, occurs. This argument doubtlessly reveals the truth that a democracy hinges upon a similarity among individual decisions. However, no optimist can be sure that such attempts at assimilation always succeed; an attempt to establish a consensus might sometimes result in failure. In cases of failure, a democracy or a nontrivial social decision function based on piecemeal comparison is confronted by a paradox.

However, we cannot overemphasize that the success

of a nontrivial social decision function depends upon the degree of similarity among individual decisions. For example, if the individual decisions are sufficiently similar as in Fig. 3, the reader can easily verify that any democratic social decision function can always provide a transitive social decision.

order of
preference

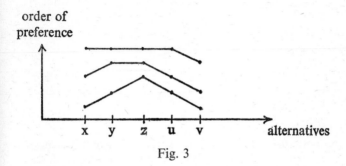

Fig. 3

But this similarity is, in fact, excessively strong for dissolving the paradox.

A classical example of the weaker, but still sufficient, similarity is presented by Duncan Black. Black's similarity notion may be called a *strong single-peakedness*, because it requires that every individual decision can be graphically represented as a single-peaked mountain on some suitable choice of an arrangement of alternatives. Fig. 4 shows all the possible profiles satisfying the strong single-peakedness assumption.

Two slopes, one upward, one downward, may be regarded as a truncated single peak. Three examples of single peaks are presented to show that the peaks may be located anywhere. It must be noted that, under

121

Black's strong single-peakedness, the curves are not allowed to be horizontal anywhere; a peak, in particular, must be pointed.

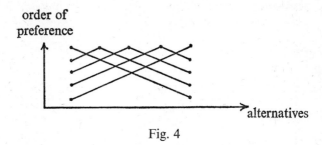

order of
preference

alternatives

Fig. 4

It turns out that Black's strong single-peakedness is still a little too strong for removing the paradox. K. J. Arrow introduced a notion of single-peakedness which allows the curves to consist of two points at a peak, and is otherwise equivalent to Black's notion. In logical terms, Arrow's notion is formulated as follows. An arrangement of alternatives may be expressed by a strong ordering S. (The arrangement of alternatives in Fig. 1 or 2 is expressed as xSy and ySz.)

Definition (single-peaked preference): There exists an arrangement of alternatives expressed by a strong ordering S, such that, for every j, and for every triple alternatives (x, y, z), xR_jy, xSy and ySz implies yP_jz, and xR_jy, zSy and ySx implies yP_jz:

$$(\exists S)(j)(x)(y)(z)\{[xR_jy \,.\, \{(xSy \,.\, ySz) \\ \lor (zSy \,.\, ySx)\}] \supset yP_jz\}$$

122

Voting Paradox Reconsidered

The following illustration exhausts the possible profiles of individual decision satisfying *single-peakedness*.

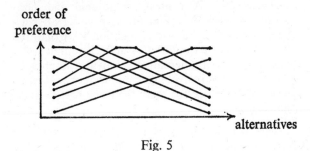

Fig. 5

It must be noted that the curves are not allowed to be horizontal anywhere below the peak.

We are now going to construct, with the aid of the single-peakedness assumption, a social decision function satisfying the axiom of ordering and Conditions 2 ~ 5. For convenience of exposition, let us define:

Condition 1″: For every combination of individual decisions satisfying the axiom of ordering and the single-peakedness assumption, the corresponding social decision satisfies the axiom of ordering.

Following Black's effort, Arrow proved:

Theorem 6–4: (Black's theorem): The rule of pairwise simple majority voting is a social decision function satisfying Condition 1″, Condition 2, Condition 3, Condition 4 and Condition 5 for any number of alternatives, provided that the number of individuals is odd.

I   123

This theorem is, in fact, a special case of the following theorem:

> *Theorem* 6–5: A neutral, monotonic and non-dictatorial social decision function based on pair-wise comparison satisfies Condition $1''$, Condition 2, Condition 3, Condition 4 and Condition 5 for any number of alternatives, provided that each combination of individual decisions does not yield a social indifference for more than one pair of alternatives.

Proof: We already know that the function of the above qualifications satisfies Conditions $2 \sim 5$. We have only to prove the transitivity of social decision. Before entering the main proof, let us prove the following preliminary lemma: Suppose that a social decision function is neutral, monotonic and based on pairwise comparison. Then, if $D_j(x, y) \geq D_j(u, v)$ for all j, $D(x, y) \geq D(u, v)$. For, by virtue of neutrality, $D_j(x, y) = D'_j(u, v)$ for all j implies $D(x, y) = D'(u, v)$. Then, if $D_j(x, y) = D'_j(u, v) \geq D_j(u, v)$ for all j, $D(x, y) = D'(u, v) \geq D(u, v)$ by virtue of monotonicity. Now we consider three possibilities.

(*a*) The alternatives are arranged as xSy and ySz, or zSy and ySx; in other words, y is situated between x and z. Suppose that xRy and yRz. Consider those individuals for whom xR_jy. By the single-peakedness assumption, xR_jy implies yP_jz. By the transitivity of individual decisions, xP_jz holds for those individuals for whom xR_jy. Then, by our preliminary lemma, xRz holds so that a transitivity of social decision is obtained.

(*b*) The alternatives are arranged as ySx and xSz, or zSx and xSy; in other words, x is situated between

124

y and z. Suppose that xRy and yRz. Consider those individuals for whom yR_jz. Then it follows that xP_jz for them. For let us suppose zR_jx for them. By the transitivity of individual decisions, we have yR_jx. Then, by the single-peakedness assumption, yR_jx implies xP_jz. This is a contradiction. Therefore, xP_jz holds for those individuals for whom yR_jz. By our preliminary lemma, xRz holds.

(*c*) The alternatives are arranged as xSz and zSy, or ySz and zSx; in other words, z is situated between x and y. Again suppose that xRy and yRz. Consider those individuals for whom yR_jz. Then, by the single-peakedness assumption, yR_jz implies zP_jx. By our preliminary lemma, zRx holds. On the other hand, by the transitivity of individual decisions, yP_jx holds for those individuals for whom yR_jz. Then, by our preliminary lemma, yRx holds. By taking the logical counterpart, zP_jy for those individuals for whom xR_jy. Then, by our preliminary lemma, zRy holds. As a whole, it follows that xIy and yIz. This contradicts our proviso, so this third case cannot occur. *Q.E.D.*

The proviso at the end of Theorem 6–5 is essential. An example in Fig. 1 gives a counter-example, in which the individual decisions satisfy the single-peakedness assumption, but the intransitivity of social decision occurs. It is easy to see that the example violates our proviso. Two corollaries are immediate. Let us consider a quasi-resolute function which we introduced in Chapter One.

Theorem 6–6: A neutral, monotonic and non-dictatorial social decision function based on pairwise comparison satisfies Condition 1″, Condition 2, Condition 3, Condition 4 and Condition 5 for any number of alternatives, provided that it is quasi-resolute.

Proof: Suppose that, for some triple of alternatives (x, y, z), xIy and yIz hold. By quasi-resoluteness, this implies xI_jy and yI_jz for any j belonging to a certain group of individuals. But this contradicts the single-peakedness assumption. *Q.E.D.*

Quasi-resoluteness is a kind of generalization of chairman's rule. If a chairman at the supreme council is given the right to break a social indifference, any combination of simple majority voting based on pairwise comparison and sufficiently similar individual decisions always yields a transitive social decision. Another corollary is Theorem 6–4 which concerns simple majority voting.

Theorem 6–4 (Black's theorem): The rule of simple majority voting based on pairwise comparison satisfies Condition 1″, Condition 2, Condition 3, Condition 4 and Condition 5 for any number of alternatives, provided that the number of individuals is odd.

Proof: Evidently we have only to consider case (c) in the proof of Theorem 6–5. Suppose that xIz and zIy hold. Consider those individuals for whom xI_jz. By the single-peakedness assumption, zP_jy holds for them. By the nature of simple majority voting, zRy holds and, moreover, zPy holds, if there exist individuals for whom xI_jz and zP_jy hold. Therefore, there cannot exist individuals for whom xI_jz holds. Then, xIz implies, by the nature of simple majority voting, that the number of the individuals for whom xP_jz and the number of the individuals for whom zP_jx holds are equal. This means that the number of the individuals is even. This contradicts our proviso. *Q.E.D.*

The example in Fig. 1 shows that the proviso of an odd number of individuals is essential to the theorem.

As a matter of fact, the single-peakedness assumption is only one example of the similarities among individual decisions that can guarantee a transitive social decision. For example, the geometrical converse of single-peakedness can play the same role.

Definition (single-valleyedness):

$$(\exists S)(j)(x)(y)(z)\{[xR_jy \cdot \{(xSy \cdot ySz) \vee (zSy \cdot ySx)\}] \\ \supset zP_jy\}$$

The single-valleyedness assumption is sufficient to establish the theorem corresponding to Theorem 6–6. The proof being exactly analogous is left to the reader.

Inada has been trying to discover the similarity conditions, including the single-valleyedness assumption and others, that can guarantee a transitive social decision. Moreover, he recently succeeded in enumerating exhaustively all those similarity conditions. Some of his conditions are difficult to interpret in sociological terms, but others are suggestive.

This section has been concerned with those similarity conditions which are powerful enough to guarantee a transitivity of social decision. Those similarity conditions are, no doubt, of crucial importance to the problem of social decision-making, whether theoretical or empirical. However, some weaker similarity conditions are also relevant to the present problem, in that they can give some minor assistance to a dissolution of the paradox of social decision. For example, individual consumers' decisions, represented as indifference curves, are somewhat similar in the sense that they all prefer an expenditure plan composed of larger quantities of consumption goods to another expenditure plan composed of smaller quantities. By virtue of this weak similarity, we need not go so far as overall comparison in order to dissolve the paradox of social decision. An introduction of suitable piecemeal comparison is sufficient for constructing a social decision function, though the required piecemeal comparison still involves infinitely many expenditure plans. There are many examples of the same nature as this example of a society composed of consumers. Whether strong or weak, similarity or consensus among individuals is, indeed, crucial to the paradox of social decision.

6. Relaxation of Transitivity. In the last section, we tried to relax the condition of complete freedom required of individual decisions. In this section, we shall try to relax the remaining part of Condition 1', that is, the transitivity of social decisions. To be exact, the transitivity of social decision includes four types of transitivity which are

$$(x)(y)(z)\{(xPy \cdot yPz) \supset xPz\},$$
$$(x)(y)(z)\{(xPy \cdot yIz) \supset xPz\},$$
$$(x)(y)(z)\{(xIy \cdot yPz) \supset xPz\},$$
$$(x)(y)(z)\{(xIy \cdot yIz) \supset xIz\}.$$

It was proved in Chapter One that the second and third statements are derived from the first and the last.

Let us now try to require only that a social preference be transitive, and a social indifference not be transitive; only the first statement among the above four is required to hold. In other words, Condition 1' is to be replaced by:

Condition 1''': For all combinations of individual

decisions satisfying three axioms of ordering, the corresponding social decision shall satisfy Axioms 1 and 2, but not necessarily Axiom 3.

It must be noted that no circular ordering occurs under Axioms 1 and 2. Indeed, the alternatives cannot be partitioned into the equivalence classes, as under Axioms 1 $\sim$ 3. But any other irregularity cannot occur. Particularly, we have to note that, under normal conditions, Condition 1''' implies an existence of an outcome of the individual decisions. The trouble with intransitive social preference is that there is no outcome for some combinations of individual decisions. There is no such trouble with intransitive social indifference. The present relaxation of the transitivity condition may be sufficiently acceptable.

However, this relaxation does not dissolve the paradox in question. For as is shown in the proof of general possibility theorem, say, of Theorem 5–3, a social decision function satisfying Arrow's five conditions yields an intransitive social *preference*, so that admitting intransitive social indifference does not help us at all.

However, the relaxation enables us to establish the main part of Theorem 6–5 without any proviso.

Theorem 6–7: A neutral, monotonic and nondictatorial social decision function satisfies Condition 1''', Condition 2, Condition 3, Condition 4 and Condition 5, if the single-peakedness assumption is satisfied.

Proof: Remember the proof of Theorem 6–5. Note that the proviso is necessary only for the exclusion of intransitive social indifference. *Q.E.D.*

Dummett and Farquharson established a similar theorem under a little weaker single-peakedness assumption, although their definition of 'majority decision' is different from ours and somewhat unusual. The interested reader will find their article suggestive. In view of our conclusion as well as Dummett and Farquharson's, a relaxation of collective rationality requirement seems ineffective, unless it modifies *transitivity of social preference*. However, an attempt of such modification is, as is seen in Guilbaud's effort, likely to be troublesome.

7. Welfare Economics. Our analysis in this book has established the *paradox of social decision* as an ultimate extension of voting paradox. A social decision-making is, in essence, an aggregation of many orderings called individual decisions into one ordering called a social decision. We have shown that such aggregations are, with trivial exceptions, impossible, in so far as no prior assumptions are imposed on individual decisions, and social decisions are based on piecemeal comparison. A paradox inheres in any nontrivial piecemeal attempt to aggregate individual decisions. Immune from this paradox are only such extraordinary societies as dictatorial, persecutional or traditional societies, all of which may be regarded as trivial aggregations of individual decisions. Whether a majority rules or not, almost any society is confronted with the paradox. Democracy is no longer the sole society to be blamed for inconsistent social decisions. Our conclusion is far reaching.

Moreover, we may note that our analytical framework is quite formal. Our analysis can be applied to any problem which can be formulated as a social decision-making problem, whether a 'decision-maker' is an actual machine such as voting or market mechanism, or a leader anxious to respond to the people's demands, or even a scholar counselled by the Government or similar bodies. With proper care about interpretation, our argument is quite helpful in any of these problems.

However, Arrow's pioneering work *Social Choice and Individual Values,* from which our present analysis originated, has been given a more specific interpretation in spite of Arrow's repeated elucidation. Indeed, Arrow himself formulated and analysed his problem with primary reference to economics, so that the economists associated his problem with *welfare economics,* a traditional nomenclature vaguely representing a social decision-making problem in economics. Specifically, his negative conclusion is interpreted as asserting the impossibility of welfare economic analysis. In essence, Arrow's analysis as well as ours is concerned with a wider problem than welfare economics. However, considering the circumstances in which Arrow's work was presented to the public, it would be clarifying to show here what the present analysis implies in the particular problem called welfare economics.

Welfare economics may be defined as an analysis of social decision in a society where each individual is a *consumer.* By a consumer we mean an individual who makes his decision concerning only his own expenditure plans. As an expenditure plan is composed of the quantities of the commodities to be purchased and consumed, each plan can be expressed as a point in a finite-dimensional Euclidean space, where each dimension represents a quantity of each commodity. As any textbook of economics explains, each individual's decision can be graphically represented as a so-called 'indifference map' over infinite points in such Euclidean space. An *alternative* to the society is a conceivable combination of all individuals' expenditure plans, so that an *issue* to the society is an *n*-fold Cartesian product of the commodity space conceived above. The issue obviously includes infinitely many alternatives.

Let us now recall our argument in Section 3 of this chapter. Welfare economic judgement, or a social decision faced with this welfare economic situation, can be always consistent, if a 'decision-maker' can achieve an overall comparison. However, it should here be noted, as we did at the end of Section 5, that several prior restrictions are, in ordinary economic analysis, imposed on each consumer's indifference map. For example, each consumer is supposed to prefer an expenditure plan composed of larger quantities of commodities to that composed of smaller quantities. By virtue of this prior information, a rational welfare economic judgement can be made on a piecemeal basis. But such piecemeal comparison still involves infinitely many alternatives. Welfare economic judgement has to collect the information about individual decisions concerning infinitely many expenditure plans, or, more visually, about the shape of infinitely many indifference curves of each consumer.

Many economists seem to assume implicitly that the entire pattern of every individual's indifference map is fully known to the 'decision-maker' or to the welfare economist. If the economist is really brave enough to assume that the 'decision-maker' is omniscient in this sense, consistent welfare economic judgement is no difficulty at all. However, as we argued before, a collection of an infinite amount of information must be regarded as *un-workable*, though logically possible. Therefore, welfare economic judgement based on such information is un-workable in our sense; an omniscient 'decision-maker' is obviously an un-workable notion.

We may assert that we cannot *actually* aggregate all consumers' indifference maps into a social decision which is always consistent. Welfare economic judgement is workable, if at all, only as a piecemeal decision. In fact, market mechanism can be regarded as a social decision-making rule for performing such piecemeal aggregation, though the 'decision-maker' is not explicitly embodied. Everybody knows that market mechanism cannot guarantee overall consistency. Welfare economics is, after all, not meaningful as an actual advisory science, but is useful as a deductive analysis originating from several idealized assumptions, in other words, only as an *axiomatics*.

As is shown in this particular case of welfare economics, a basic way to dissolve the paradox of social decision is the introduction of an overall comparison. A social decision must be made once and for all on the entire issue. However, the concept of *issue* is, more or less, relative. For any specified issue, we can ordinarily conceive a larger issue which includes some additional alternatives. An overall comparison in some issue may well be a piecemeal comparison in some larger issue. A dissolution of the paradox of social decision is subject to this limitation.

All in all, we may conclude that the dissolution of the paradox of social decision is, if not logically impossible, hardly workable in many significant cases. This conclusion may be disturbing to some people. However, we must recall that our human activities are always piecemeal, and piecemeal rationality never ensures overall rationality. The paradox of social decision may be regarded as another symptom of such human imperfection. We cannot help relying on 'piecemeal engineering' as K. R. Popper called it. A society is, after all, the product of piecemeal efforts which are deemed optimal on each occasion.

Suggested Reading

Arrow, K. J.: *Social Choice and Individual Values*, 2nd edn. (1964)

Black, D.: *The Theory of Committees and Elections* (1958)

Buchanan, J. M. & G. TULLOCK: *The Calculus of Consent* (1962)

Chipman, J. S.: 'The Foundations of Utility', *Econometrica* (1960)

Dahl, R.: *A Preface to Democratic Theory* (1956)

Davidson, D. & P. Suppes: *Decision Making* (1957)

Downs, A.: *An Economic Theory of Democracy* (1957)

Dummett, M. & R. Farquharson: 'Stability in Voting', *Econometrica* (1961)

Friedman, M. & L. J. Savage: 'The Utility Analysis of Choices Involving Risk', *Journal of Political Economy* (1948)

Guilbaud, G. T.: 'Les Théories de L'intérêt Général et la Problème Logique de L'agrégation', *Economie Appliquée* (1952)

Hildreth, C.: 'Alternative Conditions for Social Orderings', *Econometrica* (1953)

Inada, K.: 'A Note on the Simple Majority Rule',
    Econometrica (1964)
Inada, K.: 'On the Economic Welfare Function',
    Econometrica (1964)
Luce, R. D. & H. Raiffa: *Games and Decisions* (1957)
Mosteller, F. & P. Nogee: 'An Experimental Measure-
    ment of Utility', *Journal of Political Economy*
    (1951)
Rothenberg, J.: *The Measurement of Social Welfare*
    (1961)